FEAR THE SPEAR
FLORIDA STATE'S RETURN TO THE TOP

www.whitman.com

Fear the Spear: Florida State's Return to the Top

Excluding certain works, whose copyright may or may not be noted, ©2014 Whitman Publishing, LLC
3101 Clairmont Road · Suite G · Atlanta GA 30329

Excluding certain works, whose copyright may or may not be noted, all rights reserved, including duplication of any kind and storage in electronic or visual retrieval systems. Permission is granted for writers to use a reasonable number of brief excerpts and quotations in printed reviews and articles, provided credit is given to the title of the work and the publisher. Written permission from the publisher is required for other uses of text, illustrations and other content, including in books and electronic or other media.

Florida State University® logos, emblems, symbols and insignia are licensed with permission of The Collegiate Licensing Company. The names, logos, emblems, symbols and insignia of Florida State University® are the property of Florida State University®.

The Coaches' Trophy and images of the Crystal Football are trademarks of the American Football Coaches Association (AFCA). The AFCA is the copyright owner of The Coaches' Trophy©, The Symbol of Supremacy in College Football.™ 1986 AFCA®

Correspondence concerning this book may be directed to the publisher, at the address above.

ISBN: 0794842291
Printed and assembled in the United States.

This book is authorized by Florida State University®. Whitman Publishing, LLC, and Florida State University® are not necessarily endorsed by or connected with any of the organizations or entities featured herein.

To view other products by Whitman Publishing, please visit **www.Whitman.com**.

TABLE OF CONTENTS

INTRODUCTION..4
GAME 1: FLORIDA STATE AT PITTSBURGH....................6
GAME 2: FLORIDA STATE VS NEVADA........................14
GAME 3: FLORIDA STATE VS BETHUNE-COOKMAN...22
GAME 4: FLORIDA STATE AT BOSTON COLLEGE........30
GAME 5: FLORIDA STATE VS MARYLAND....................38
GAME 6: FLORIDA STATE AT CLEMSON.......................46
GAME 7: FLORIDA STATE VS NC STATE.......................54
GAME 8: FLORIDA STATE VS MIAMI............................62
GAME 9: FLORIDA STATE AT WAKE FOREST..............70
GAME 10: FLORIDA STATE VS SYRACUSE...................78
GAME 11: FLORIDA STATE VS IDAHO..........................86
GAME 12: FLORIDA STATE AT FLORIDA.....................94
GAME 13: FLORIDA STATE VS DUKE.........................102
GAME 14: FLORIDA STATE VS AUBURN....................114
ACKNOWLEDGEMENTS...144

The 2013 National Champion Florida State Seminoles

When Jimbo Fisher took over as head coach of the Florida State football program in 2010, his goal was "to facilitate a winning plan." That plan came to fruition when the Seminoles won the BCS National Championship Game at the end of the 2013 season, taking home The Coaches' Trophy — the symbol of supremacy in college football. It was the first national title for FSU since 1999.

This book covers the perfect 14-0 campaign, from the season-opening victory over Pitt to the thrilling, come-from-behind 34-31 win over Auburn in Pasadena. On the pages that follow, you will see over 100 photographs illustrating FSU's championship season and game-by-game coverage provided by Florida State Athletic Media Relations.

	Florida State Football 2013-14		
09/02/13	at Pittsburgh	Pittsburgh	W 41-13
09/14/13	vs. Nevada	Tallahassee	W 62-7
09/21/13	vs. Bethune-Cookman	Tallahassee	W 54-6
09/28/13	at Boston College	Chestnut Hill	W 48-34
10/05/13	vs. Maryland	Tallahassee	W 63-0
10/19/13	at Clemson	Clemson	W 51-14
10/26/13	vs. North Carolina State	Tallahassee	W 49-17
11/02/13	vs. Miami	Tallahassee	W 41-14
11/09/13	at Wake Forest	Winston-Salem	W 59-3
11/16/13	vs. Syracuse	Tallahassee	W 59-3
11/23/13	vs. Idaho	Tallahassee	W 80-14
11/30/13	at Florida	Gainesville	W 37-7
	ACC Championship Game		
12/07/13	vs. Duke	Charlotte	W 45-7
	BCS National Championship Game		
01/06/14	vs. Auburn	Pasadena, CA	W 34-31

GAME 1 • SEPT. 2, 2013

FLORIDA STATE 41
PITTSBURGH 13

	1	2	3	4	F
Florida State	7	21	6	7	41
Pittsburgh	7	3	3	0	13

He had thrown fastballs in the 90s and runners out at third base from right field. He'd thrown a touchdown on his first toss of the 2013 spring game and he'd thrown a football up and over a fraternity house. He'd even joked with reporters and debuted a flawless MC Hammer impersonation.

But there was one thing Jameis Winston hadn't done in a whirlwind, hype-producing eight months: Florida State's redshirt freshman quarterback hadn't played a single snap of college football. So when the nation turned its collective gaze to ESPN's Labor Day broadcast of No. 11 FSU's season-opening game at Pittsburgh, the game's central theme was crystal clear.

Can the player they call "Jaboo" live up to the hype?

If the box score from the Seminoles' 41-13 thrashing of new ACC member Pitt is any indication, Winston appears more than capable of handling the pressures of his growing fame and expectations.

In what may be the single greatest debut by a 'Noles quarterback ever, Winston went 25 of 27 for 356 yards with four passing touchdowns and one rushing score. His 92.6-percent completion percentage was enough to set the school record, breaking the 87.5-percent mark Danny Kanell unleashed on N.C. State in 1995.

Not to be overlooked was an FSU offense that saw Nick O'Leary match his 2012 full-season total with three touchdown receptions and become the first Seminoles tight end to haul in more than one score in a single game since Melvin Pearsall in 1994.

Rashad Greene had eight catches for 126 yards and one score, and Kelvin Benjamin added 73 yards on five catches. Kenny Shaw nearly hit triple digits with his 94 yards on four catches while tailbacks James Wilder Jr. and Devonta Freeman combined for 110 yards on 19 carries.

The Seminoles racked up 533 yards of total offense on 8.5 yards per play. With Winston effortlessly running head coach Jimbo Fisher's pro-style offense, the 'Noles were 7 of 11 on third down.

Defensively, the new-look 'Noles bent early but they didn't break. FSU allowed just 297 yards while forcing Pitt quarterback Tom Savage to throw two interceptions — one by true freshman starting cornerback Jalen Ramsey and another by senior safety Terrence Brooks.

The Seminoles allowed an 80-yard drive and score to start the game, but gave up just 217 yards and six points over the next 49:10 of game action.

Lamarcus Joyner had a role in the pressure, as the senior registered two sacks off the cornerback blitz and led the team with nine tackles.

Savage orchestrated that nine-play drive on the first series that concluded with a 4-yard touchdown pass to Manasseh Garner.

The Winston era then officially began with back-to-back completions to Benjamin and Shaw for a combined 33 yards. But the drive stalled after Benjamin's toss sweep failed to convert on third-and-1.

After Cason Beatty's first punt of the season, Pittsburgh's ensuing drive fared much worse. With 'Noles

defensive line pressure in his face, Savage threw a pass right into Ramsey's waiting hands. Two plays later, Winston tossed the first touchdown of his career on a beautifully thrown 24-yard pass to O'Leary.

A perfectly executed play-action pass with defensive tackle Jacobbi McDaniel in as a lead blocker then resulted in another Winston to O'Leary touchdown connection — this time a 2-yard score for a 14-7 FSU lead with 13:41 left in the second quarter.

Pitt then trimmed that one-touchdown deficit to 14-10 on a short field goal moments after Brooks' nearly snared an end zone interception.

But a 14-play, 78-yard drive by the Winston-led offense halted any sort of potential Panthers comeback. The drive concluded with Winston's first career rushing touchdown, a 5-yard scamper with 2:13 remaining in the first half.

Brooks made up for his dropped interception earlier by making a diving takeaway for Savage's second pick. Wasting little time, Winston led the 'Noles to paydirt once again. Highlighted by a 36-yard Greene catch on first and 30, the three-play, 41-yard drive ended with Greene's own 23-yard reception for a 28-10 halftime lead.

Roberto Aguayo hit 22- and 28-yard field goals in the third quarter, and Winston capped off the night with a 10-yard touchdown toss to O'Leary with 9:32 left in the game.

SCORING SUMMARY

First Quarter
UP 10:50 TD Garner 4-yd pass (Blewitt kick)
FS 4:11   TD O'Leary 24-yd pass (Aguayo kick)

Second Quarter
FS 13:41 TD O'Leary 2-yd pass (Aguayo kick)
UP 9:18   FG Blewitt 28-yd
FS 2:13   TD Winston 5-yd rush (Aguayo kick)
FS :38   TD Greene 23-yd pass (Aguayo kick)

Third Quarter
FS 11:08 FG Aguayo 22-yd
UP 4:43   FG Blewitt 39-yd
FS 1:12   FG Aguayo 28-yd

Fourth Quarter
FS 9:32   TD O'Leary 10-yd pass (Aguayo kick)

FLORIDA STATE STATS

Passing
Name	Comp-Att-Int	Yards	TD
Jameis Winston	25-27-0	356	4
Jacob Coker	2-2-0	21	0
Total	27-29-0	377	4

Rushing
Name	Att-Yards	Avg	TD
James Wilder Jr.	10-58	5.8	0
Devonta Freeman	9-52	5.8	0
Jameis Winston	8-25	3.1	1
Chad Abram	2-13	6.5	0
Ryan Green	5-8	1.6	0
Total	34-156	4.6	1

Receiving
Name	Att-Yards	Avg	TD
Rashad Greene	8-126	15.8	1
Kenny Shaw	4-94	23.5	0
Kelvin Benjamin	5-73	14.6	0
Nick O'Leary	4-47	11.8	3
Isaiah Jones	1-15	15.0	0
Chad Abram	2-11	5.5	0
Devonta Freeman	2-11	5.5	0
Christian Green	1-0	0.0	0
Total	27-377	14.0	4

GAME 1 · SEPT. 2, 2013

■ Quarterback Jameis Winston (5) follows his blockers on a 5-yard touchdown run.

■ Rashad Greene catches one of his eight receptions for 126 yards and a touchdown against Pitt.

Tight end Nick O'Leary with one of his three touchdown catches on the day.

GAME 1 · SEPT. 2, 2013

■ The FSU defense brings down a Pitt runner.

■ James Wilder Jr. finds a hole in the Panther defensive line.

FLORIDA STATE 41 · PITTSBURGH 13

Jalen Ramsey prepares to bring down a Pitt runner.

GAME 1 · SEPT. 2, 2013

Devonta Freeman makes a cut.

Fullback Chad Abram averaged 6.5 yards per carry against Pittsburgh.

GAME 2 • SEPT. 14, 2013

FLORIDA STATE 62
NEVADA 7

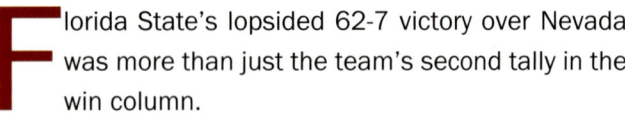

	1	2	3	4	F
Nevada	0	7	0	0	7
Florida State	3	14	31	14	62

Florida State's lopsided 62-7 victory over Nevada was more than just the team's second tally in the win column.

The Seminoles' triumphant 2013 home opener also provided answers to some key offensive questions moving forward.

With a record-breaking debut in his rearview mirror, freshman quarterback Jameis Winston had yet to show what he could do when things weren't going right. Against Pitt in the 'Noles' season opener, Winston had just two incompletions and, other than briefly playing from behind at the very beginning of the game, was never put in position to show his mental makeup in the face of adversity.

Against the Wolf Pack, he got that chance.

After throwing his first career interception and more incompletions in the first quarter at Doak Campbell Stadium than he did in all four quarters against the Panthers, Winston found his team trailing 7-3 in the second quarter in front of an unhappy crowd. As he came to the sideline, FSU coach Jimbo Fisher had a simple message for his young pupil.

"Go higher," Winston recalled Fisher saying. "Adversity is here; how are you going to respond?"

A final stat-line of 15 of 18 for 214 yards and three total touchdowns as the 'Noles scored 59 unanswered points means that Winston responded by completing all 13 of his final passes for 184 yards following Fisher's brief words of advice.

"Adversity, you can't live on that," said Winston. "You've got to keep going."

And keep going he did. Aided by his playmaking wide receivers, a stable of capable tailbacks and the blocking up front, Winston connected on a pair of 24-yard touchdown passes to Kenny Shaw and Rashad Greene in the second quarter that put the Seminoles ahead for good.

His pinpoint pass to Christian Green moments after the Shaw touchdown grab that set up Greene's score was the type of throw that won't soon be forgotten. And his 10-yard scamper to pay dirt on the heels of a third-quarter Tyler Hunter interception further proved the threat he poses as a passer and runner.

In total, FSU's offense racked up 617 yards at a clip of 9.8 yards per play while the defense allowed just 214 yards at 3.5 yards per Nevada snap.

On the ground, juniors Karlos Williams and Devonta Freeman ran for 110 and 109 yards, respectively, with one touchdown each, while true freshman Ryan Green added 78 late-game yards and one touchdown. Freshman Freddie Stevenson also had a rushing touchdown. Shaw added 94 yards and his touchdown grab, while Greene and Kelvin Benjamin combined for 76 yards and a touchdown.

On the other side of the ball, Terrence Brooks and Lamarcus Joyner both had six tackles as 24 different defenders registered stops.

"We dealt with adversity very well, we adjusted on the sideline well," said Fisher. "I loved the way our players responded. A lot of young guys touched the ball tonight. Defensively a lot of guys got in the game and made plays."

That included Williams, who made news during FSU's bye week thanks to a position switch from safety to running back.

While Winston's ability to handle adversity was the prevailing question entering the showdown with the Wolf Pack, Williams' role as a runner was the other. But after spending two seasons as a backup safety before being added to a depth chart that already featured proven players in Freeman and James Wilder Jr., Williams wasted little time in showing just what he brings to the tailback rotation: speed, size and explosion. Oh, and the ability to score from anywhere on the field.

Williams' first carry went for 65 yards and a touchdown on a sweep to the right that he had been working on all week at practice.

"Kelvin (Benjamin) and Rashad (Greene) looked at me and said, 'When you catch the ball, bro, just ride. Just run. Just run, run, run, run, run. Don't look back, don't cut, don't shake. Get the ball, head to the sideline and just run,'" said Williams. "And I did exactly what they told me and it led me to a touchdown."

SCORING SUMMARY

First Quarter
FS 6:19 FG Aguayo 23-yd

Second Quarter
NEV 11:31 TD Wimberly 11-yd pass (Zuzo kick)
FS 3:21 TD Shaw 24-yd pass (Aguayo kick)
FS :38 TD Greene 24-yd pass (Aguayo kick)

Third Quarter
FS 14:29 TD Freeman 6-yd rush (Aguayo kick)
FS 12:47 TD Williams 65-yd rush (Aguayo kick)
FS 10:06 TD Wilder 1-yd rush (Aguayo kick)
FS 4:41 TD Winston 10-yd rush (Aguayo kick)
FS :58 FG Aguayo, 33-yd

Fourth Quarter
FS 7:11 TD Stevenson 1-yd rush (Aguayo kick)
FS 2:48 TD Green 1-yd rush (Aguayo kick)

FLORIDA STATE STATS

Passing

Name	Comp-Att-Int	Yards	TD
Jameis Winston	15-18-1	214	2
Jacob Coker	2-4-0	26	0
Total	17-22-1	240	2

Rushing

Name	Att-Yards	Avg	TD
Karlos Williams	8-110	13.8	1
Devonta Freeman	9-109	12.1	1
Ryan Green	5-78	15.6	1
James Wilder Jr.	6-45	7.5	1
Jacob Coker	1-12	12.0	0
Freddie Stevenson	3-10	3.3	1
Jameis Winston	4-8	2.0	1
Sean Maguire	1-6	6.0	0
Nigel Terrell	1-4	4.0	0
Cameron Ponder	1-0	0.0	0
Team	2-(-5)	-2.5	0
Total	41-377	9.2	6

Receiving

Name	Att-Yards	Avg	TD
Kenny Shaw	6-94	15.7	1
Rashad Greene	3-39	13.0	1
Kelvin Benjamin	2-37	18.5	0
Christian Green	1-19	19.0	0
Nick O'Leary	2-16	8.0	0
Kermit Whitfield	1-16	16.0	0
Freddie Stevenson	1-10	10.0	0
James Wilder Jr.	1-9	9.0	0
Total	17-240	14.1	2

GAME 2 · SEPT. 14, 2013

Karlos Williams, who was moved from safety to running back after the season opener, breaks free on a 65-yard touchdown run against Nevada.

FLORIDA STATE 62 · NEVADA 7

Devonta Freeman turns the corner during a 109-yard rushing day.

GAME 2 · SEPT. 14, 2013

■ Jameis Winston threw two touchdown passes against Nevada and ran for another.

■ Ryan Green busts loose for a few of his 78 rushing yards.

FLORIDA STATE 62 • NEVADA 7

■ Tyler Hunter returns an interception.

■ FSU's offensive line dominated the Wolf Pack defense, as six Seminoles scored rushing touchdowns.

GAME 2 · SEPT. 14, 2013

■ Tyler Hunter puts a big hit on the Nevada quarterback.

■ Osceola and Renegade celebrated eight Florida State touchdowns on the day.

FLORIDA STATE 62 · NEVADA 7

Karlos Williams gets a fist bump from head coach Jimbo Fisher during the 62-7 victory.

GAME 3 • SEPT. 21, 2013

FLORIDA STATE 54
BETHUNE-COOKMAN 6

	1	2	3	4	F
Bethune-Cookman	0	0	6	0	6
Florida State	10	23	21	0	54

Telvin Smith intercepted a pass and dashed 68 yards for the touchdown on the game's first drive and No. 8 Florida State sprinted past Bethune-Cookman 54-6.

Unlike the first two games of his career, FSU quarterback Jameis Winston didn't fill up the box score with eye-popping numbers in the win. But the young signal caller did make some magic.

Winston only played until the 8:13 mark of the third quarter, completing 10 of 19 passes for 148 yards and two touchdowns. Don't let the numbers fool you, though. Winston had two potential touchdown tosses dropped, and he unleashed an 11-yard touchdown throw to Kelvin Benjamin that won't soon be forgotten.

Winston admitted that the memorable play shouldn't have ever happened; he should have hit Chad Abram in the flat or Nick O'Leary on a hot route. But you can't take those points off the board and that play off of the ESPN highlight reels.

Rashad Greene also grabbed a 19-yard touchdown catch from Winston. Greene finished with 44 yards receiving on four catches, while Kenny Shaw had four catches of his own for 89 yards. Kermit Whitfield added one catch for 42 yards from backup quarterback Jacob Coker.

Of FSU's 492 total yards, 266 of them came on the ground.

Devonta Freeman registered his second 100-yard game in a row, and the sixth of his career, as his 10 total rushes went for 112 yards and one touchdown.

The other members of the 'Noles' talented tailback trio — James Wilder Jr. and Karlos Williams — also left their mark. Wilder finished with 56 yards and a touchdown on just eight carries, and Williams showed the same flash in the backfield as he did in his first game at the position after his switch from safety. Williams only played in the second half but ran for 83 yards and two scores on nine carries. He also laid out a Wildcats' returner on special teams, showing he hadn't forgotten how to notch one of his trademark hits despite his position switch from defense.

The Seminoles averaged 8.1 yards per play, and FSU's defense let Bethune-Cookman gain just 242 yards.

Starting for the first time in his career, linebacker Terrance Smith showed off with a game-high 12 tackles and one sack. Redshirt freshmen Chris Casher and Ukeme Eligwe added 10 and six tackles, respectively, while E.J. Levenberry, Reggie Northrup, Telvin Smith and Terrence Brooks all had five stops apiece. Freshmen Jalen Ramsey and Matthew Thomas each added three tackles and a sack.

The 'Noles started slow defensively, giving up four B-CU first downs on the opening drive before Terrance Smith's big second-down sack set up a third-and-16 play. Telvin Smith then stepped in front the pass and raced untouched for the Seminoles' first defensive score of the year and a 7-0 lead.

It took until the 4:31 mark of the first quarter for the FSU offense to get the ball for the first time. Freeman's

18-yard run, a 14-yard Benjamin catch and a 24-yard Shaw grab set up a 45-yard Roberto Aguayo field goal for a 10-0 score.

After Wilder's fumble near the goal line, B-CU quickly gave the ball right back with a holding penalty that resulted in a safety and a 12-0 FSU lead. Then on FSU's ensuing drive, Winston unleashed his 11-yard touchdown play to Benjamin to give the 'Noles a 19-0 advantage.

That lead extended to 26-0 late in the second quarter after Wilder found redemption with a 2-yard touchdown plunge after an 82-yard drive. FSU added one more score — a 1-yard Freeman run — before halftime to take a 33-0 lead.

Winston's 19-yard pass to Greene just 1:21 into the second half then gave FSU a 40-0 lead. The scoring play was Winston's final play before Coker took over.

Following a B-CU scoring drive that halted the would-be shutout, Coker fired a 29-yard completion to Shaw and then Williams burst for a 19-yard gain. One play later, Williams scored his second rushing TD in as many games with a 3-yard rumble for a 47-6 score.

Williams later added a 1-yard late-third-quarter run that was set up by Whitfield's 42-yard grab and dash.

SCORING SUMMARY

First Quarter
| FS | 8:39 | TD | Telvin Smith 68-yd INT (Aguayo kick) |
| FS | 2:33 | FG | Aguayo 45-yd |

Second Quarter
FS	13:50	SAF	Team -4-yd
FS	12:11	TD	Benjamin 11-yd pass (Aguayo kick)
FS	5:49	TD	Wilder 2-yd rush (Aguayo kick)
FS	1:13	TD	Freeman 1 yd rush (Aguayo kick)

Third Quarter
FS	13:39	TD	Greene 19-yd pass (Aguayo kick)
BCU	8:21	TD	Wilson 7-yd rush
FS	6:15	TD	Williams 3-yd rush (Aguayo kick)
FS	:46	TD	Williams 1 yd rush (Aguayo kick)

FLORIDA STATE STATS

Passing
Name	Comp-Att-Int	Yards	TD
Jameis Winston	10-19-0	148	2
Jacob Coker	3-6-0	78	0
Total	13-25-0	226	2

Rushing
Name	Att-Yards	Avg	TD
Devonta Freeman	10-112	11.2	1
Karlos Williams	9-83	9.2	2
James Wilder Jr.	8-56	7.0	1
Jameis Winston	3-11	3.7	0
Ryan Green	5-8	1.6	0
Jacob Coker	1-(-4)	-4.0	0
Total	36-266	7.4	4

Receiving
Name	Att-Yards	Avg	TD
Kenny Shaw	4-89	22.3	0
Rashad Greene	4-44	11.0	1
Kermit Whitfield	1-42	42.0	0
Kelvin Benjamin	2-26	13.0	1
Christian Green	2-25	12.5	0
Total	13-226	17.4	2

Telvin Smith breaks free on a 68-yard interception return in the first quarter against Bethune-Cookman.

FLORIDA STATE 54 • BETHUNE-COOKMAN 6

James Wilder Jr. fights for extra yardage.

Kermit Whitfield is off to the races against B-CU.

GAME 3 · SEPT. 21, 2013

■ Christian Green fights off a defender after the catch.

■ The Florida State defense swarms to a Bethune-Cookman ball carrier.

FLORIDA STATE 54 · BETHUNE-COOKMAN 6

James Wilder Jr. fights for extra yardage.

Kermit Whitfield is off to the races against B-CU.

GAME 3 · SEPT. 21, 2013

■ Christian Green fights off a defender after the catch.

■ The Florida State defense swarms to a Bethune-Cookman ball carrier.

FLORIDA STATE 54 · BETHUNE-COOKMAN 6

James Wilder Jr. fights for extra yardage.

Kermit Whitfield is off to the races against B-CU.

GAME 3 · SEPT. 21, 2013

■ Christian Green fights off a defender after the catch.

■ The Florida State defense swarms to a Bethune-Cookman ball carrier.

FLORIDA STATE 54 · BETHUNE-COOKMAN 6

James Wilder Jr. fights for extra yardage.

Kermit Whitfield is off to the races against B-CU.

GAME 3 · SEPT. 21, 2013

■ Christian Green fights off a defender after the catch.

■ The Florida State defense swarms to a Bethune-Cookman ball carrier.

FLORIDA STATE 54 · BETHUNE-COOKMAN 6

Devonta Freeman delivers a blow to a B-CU defender. Freeman led all rushers with 112 yards.

Kelvin Benjamin tries to catch a Jameis Winston pass.

FLORIDA STATE 54 • BETHUNE-COOKMAN 6

■ Jameis Winston tries to avoid a B-CU tackler.

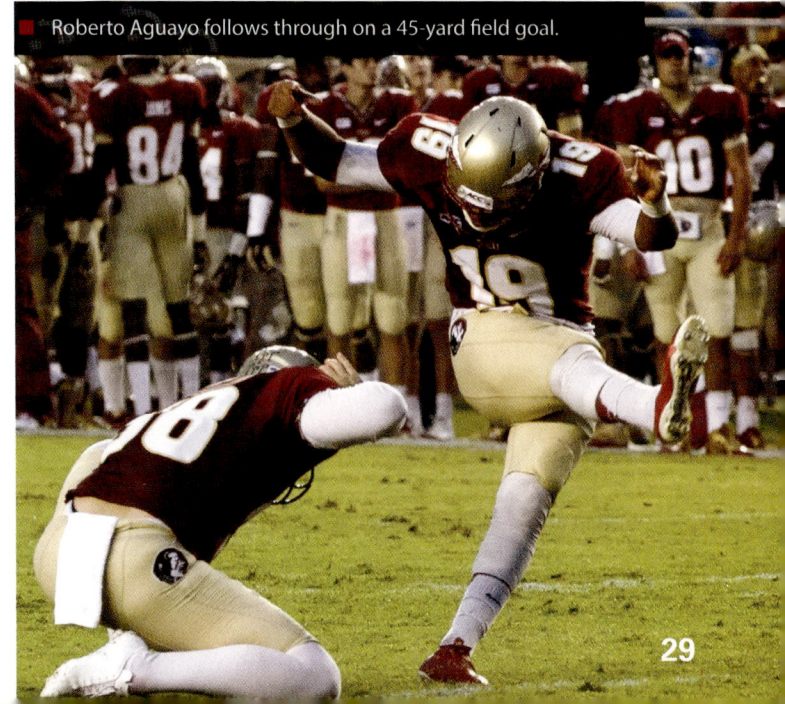

■ Roberto Aguayo follows through on a 45-yard field goal.

29

GAME 4 • SEPT. 28, 2013

FLORIDA STATE 48
BOSTON COLLEGE 34

	1	2	3	4	F
Florida State	3	21	14	10	48
Boston College	14	3	10	7	34

No. 8 Florida State's defense bent but didn't break, while Jameis Winston bent his way out of two potential sacks on the same play and broke social media in the process during the Seminoles' come-from-behind 48-34 win at Boston College.

FSU's defense struggled to stop the run and the 'Noles fell behind 17-3 early. But when the defense started generating stops, Winston and the offense began rolling, and no play was more memorable and meaningful than the young quarterback's 55-yard touchdown throw to Kenny Shaw as the first half expired.

The play, which featured Winston calmly eluding two would-be sacks, was followed by a social media frenzy in which word — and video — of the miraculous play spread across the Internet at an eye-popping, reload-at-your-own-risk rate.

For Winston, the play was part of an eight-pass completion streak that saw him lead FSU from a two-score deficit to an advantage it would never relinquish, overcoming four Chase Rettig touchdown passes for Boston College.

Winston finished 17 of 27 for 330 yards with four touchdowns and one interception. He also added 67 yards rushing on 14 carries. His do-it-all effort propelled the Seminoles to 489 yards of total offense.

Rashad Greene hauled in two of Winston's touchdown throws and finished with 90 yards on four catches, while Kelvin Benjamin (three catches for 103 yards) and Shaw (four catches for 93 yards and a score) also put up big numbers.

Starting fullback Chad Abram also had a touchdown catch for his first career score.

Devonta Freeman added 49 yards on nine carries, and Karlos Williams posted a 1-yard touchdown run. Redshirt freshman Roberto Aguayo contributed two field goals and six extra points.

P.J. Williams' pick six early in the fourth quarter gave the Seminoles a more comfortable lead, and Nate Andrews' game-sealing takeaway at the FSU 1 with less than two minutes left kept the Eagles from making it a one-score affair. Telvin Smith contributed a big sack of Rettig that helped set up Andrews' interception on the next play.

Smith registered a team-high 10 tackles while Terrence Brooks, Timmy Jernigan, Christian Jones and Jalen Ramsey all had seven stops. Desmond Hollin and Eddie Goldman also added sacks.

Boston College scored a touchdown on its first drive to take a 7-0 lead. After a 38-yard completion from Winston to Benjamin, Aguayo hit a 40-yard field goal to make it 7-3 with 6:34 left in the first quarter.

The Eagles wouldn't go away as Rettig tossed his second touchdown on the ensuing drive to give BC a 14-3 lead at the end of the first quarter, and the Eagles extended the lead to 14 points on a field goal early in the second quarter.

Down 17-3, the FSU offense finally had an answer thanks to Winston's 56-yard touchdown toss to a wide-open Greene.

After trading punts, FSU forced a second consecutive Boston College three and out before starting a beautiful offensive drive orchestrated by Winston. Starting with three consecutive first-down passes before adding a 20-yard run, Winston capped the drive with a 10-yard scoring throw to Abram to tie the game with 4:44 left in the second quarter.

The FSU defense then forced a punt, and the 'Noles took the lead on Winston's play-of-the-year-caliber pass as the first half expired for a 24-17 advantage.

Boston College had a 71-yard kickoff return to start the third quarter, but the 'Noles' defense stiffened and only allowed a field goal.

On the next drive, Winston's completion streak ended at eight, but he found Greene for a 10-yard score and a 31-20 lead. Then, Williams extended the Seminoles' advantage to 38-20 on his 1-yard scoring plunge.

But Boston College stayed in the game as Rettig's 52-yard touchdown heave to Myles Willis trimmed the deficit to 38-27. The 'Noles then got three of those back on Aguayo's 20-yard field goal on the third play of the fourth quarter.

P.J. Williams' interception return for a score 26 seconds later pushed the lead back to 48-27, but Rettig answered with a 17-yard scoring throw. The Eagles got the ball back, but Andrews stepped in front of Rettig's pass and raced 35 yards down the sideline with 1:53 left to seal the victory.

SCORING SUMMARY

First Quarter
BC	9:58	TD	Parsons 6-yd pass (Freese kick)
FS	6:34	FG	Aguayo 40-yd
BC	1:46	TD	Sinkovec 3-yd pass (Freese kick)

Second Quarter
BC	11:19	FG	Freese 24-yd
FS	10:35	TD	Greene 56-yd pass (Aguayo kick)
FS	1:49	TD	Abram 10-yd pass (Aguayo kick)
FS	:00	TD	Shaw 55-yd pass (Aguayo kick)

Third Quarter
BC	11:52	FG	Freese 24-yd
FS	9:06	TD	Greene 10-yd pass (Aguayo kick)
FS	3:42	TD	K. Williams 1-yd rush (Aguayo kick)
BC	2:10	TD	Willis 52-yd pass (Freese kick)

Fourth Quarter
FS	14:07	FG	Aguayo 20-yd
FS	13:41	TD	P.J. Williams 20-yd INT (Aguayo kick)
BC	9:44	TD	Parsons 17-yd pass (Freese kick)

FLORIDA STATE STATS

Passing
Name	Comp-Att-Int	Yards	TD
Jameis Winston	17-27-1	330	4
Total	17-27-1	330	4

Rushing
Name	Att-Yards	Avg	TD
Jameis Winston	14-67	4.8	0
Devonta Freeman	9-49	5.4	0
Karlos Williams	6-22	3.7	1
James Wilder Jr.	6-15	2.5	0
Chad Abram	1-6	6.0	0
Total	36-159	4.4	1

Receiving
Name	Att-Yards	Avg	TD
Kelvin Benjamin	3-103	34.3	0
Kenny Shaw	4-93	23.3	1
Rashad Greene	4-90	22.5	2
James Wilder Jr.	2-18	9.0	0
Chad Abram	2-15	7.5	1
Nick O'Leary	1-14	14.0	0
Christian Green	1-(-3)	-3.0	0
Total	17-330	19.4	4

GAME 4 • SEPT. 28, 2013

- Rashad Greene (left) celebrates one of his two touchdown receptions against Boston College.

Kenny Shaw looks for room to run against the Eagles. Shaw finished with four catches for 93 yards and a touchdown.

Kelvin Benjamin eyes a Jameis Winston pass. Benjamin had three receptions for 103 yards.

GAME 4 · SEPT. 28, 2013

FLORIDA STATE 48 · BOSTON COLLEGE 34

Jameis Winston scrambles for yardage. The freshman had four touchdown passes on the day.

Running back Karlos Williams breaks an arm tackle.

FLORIDA STATE 48 · BOSTON COLLEGE 34

Nile Lawrence-Stample (99) and P.J. Williams bring down BC's Andre Williams.

GAME 5 • OCT. 5, 2013

FLORIDA STATE 63
MARYLAND 0

	1	2	3	4	F
Maryland	0	0	0	0	0
Florida State	7	14	21	21	63

Playing with a chip on its shoulder, No. 8 Florida State's defense delivered whistle-to-whistle sustained blows to No. 25 Maryland in a 63-0 win at Doak Campbell Stadium — an outcome that tied the college football record for most-lopsided victory ever over a ranked team.

As the score would indicate, the previously untested Terrapins couldn't do anything against a FSU defense that had to listen to a week's worth of negative fan and media chatter in the wake of its subpar performance at Boston College.

After allowing the Eagles to generate nearly 400 yards of offense in the come-from-behind win, the 'Noles held Maryland and its 18th-ranked offense to just 234 total yards, including a paltry 33 on the ground.

"We had to play that way, man," said FSU redshirt senior defensive tackle Jacobbi McDaniel. "As a defensive player you can't play soft no matter what. We came out with a chip; we heard the doubters. Florida State football is based on defense, and we know as a group we had to come out and prove ourselves and show the offense that we are there for those guys."

McDaniel, who knocked Maryland starter C.J. Brown out of the game for good with a vicious blast to the quarterback's chest in the second quarter, and the FSU defense held the Terps to just 2 of 15 on third-down conversions and just nine total first downs.

Speedy Maryland wide receiver Stefon Diggs, who came into the game averaging 100 yards receiving per contest, was held to just 24 yards.

"The defense I thought was the story of the day — and the special teams," said FSU coach Jimbo Fisher. "I thought they really took the show. They dominated from start to finish against some great skills guys. They (Maryland) have a great scheme, and I thought our guys covered well, rushed well, we pressured the quarterback, we hit them with great leverage on the football and tackled well."

The Terrapins didn't tackle 'Noles quarterback Jameis Winston so well when the redshirt freshman made yet another ESPN "SportsCenter" Top-10 play on his 12-yard touchdown throw to Nick O'Leary in the third quarter.

Like he did at Boston College when he shucked would-be sackers to launch a 55-yard Kenny Shaw touchdown, Winston slid his way from underneath Maryland defenders for the memorable score. So while the defense was delivering its blows, Winston was throwing haymakers en route to completing 23 of 32 passes for 393 yards and five touchdowns.

As an offense, Florida State racked up 614 total yards and picked up 33 first downs while churning out 7.5 yards per play with no turnovers.

The Seminoles led 7-0 after the first quarter, 21-0 at halftime and 42-0 after three quarters against the Terrapins.

Devonta Freeman ran for 63 yards and a score, Karlos Williams added two touchdown runs and Rashad Greene grabbed four catches for 108 yards. Shaw had 96 yards on five catches with a touchdown, and Kelvin Benjamin snatched two touchdown catches and 60 total yards. O'Leary also had two touchdown catches for an offense that excelled at spreading the football around.

"It's fun when you look at the (stats) and everybody is contributing," said Shaw. "That's what I like, is to see everybody doing well."

Speaking of doing things well, the Seminoles once again were terrific in the final moments before halftime and the first few minutes after the break. For the fifth consecutive game, FSU scored on its final possession of the first half and on its first possession of the second. Benjamin scored on a 5-yard reception with 28 seconds left in the second quarter, and O'Leary scored the first of his TDs on an 8-yard catch with 12:18 remaining in the third quarter.

"We've got to take this off week to get better," said Fisher. "Get fundamentally better, work on some of our future opponents with some things we are going to do and get ready to get on the stretch of seven straight without an off week.

"But I'm proud of where we are at so far, and we have done what we were supposed to have done and put us in position to play some good ballgames."

SCORING SUMMARY

First Quarter
FS 8:14 TD Williams 1-yd rush (Aguayo kick)

Second Quarter
FS 6:15 TD Freeman 5-yd rush (Aguayo kick)
FS :28 TD Benjamin 5-yd pass (Aguayo kick)

Third Quarter
FS 12:18 TD O'Leary 8-yd pass (Aguayo kick)
FS 9:47 TD Shaw 21-yd pass (Aguayo kick)
FS 1:50 TD O'Leary 12-yd pass (Aguayo kick)

Fourth Quarter
FS 14:56 TD Benjamin 21-yd pass (Aguayo kick)
FS 11:28 TD Williams 17-yd rush (Aguayo kick)
FS 9:49 TD Coker 24-yd rush (Aguayo kick)

FLORIDA STATE STATS

Passing

Name	Comp-Att-Int	Yards	TD
Jameis Winston	23-32-0	393	5
Jacob Coker	3-7-0	38	0
Total	26-39-0	431	5

Rushing

Name	Att-Yards	Avg	TD
Devonta Freeman	17-63	3.7	1
James Wilder Jr.	6-40	6.7	0
Karlos Williams	5-29	5.8	2
Jacob Coker	1-24	24.0	1
Jameis Winston	7-24	3.4	0
Ryan Green	4-16	4.0	0
Freddie Stevenson	2-10	5.0	0
TEAM	1-(-23)	-23.0	0
Total	43-183	4.3	4

Receiving

Name	Att-Yards	Avg	TD
Rashad Greene	4-108	27.0	0
Kenny Shaw	5-96	19.2	1
Kelvin Benjamin	5-60	12.0	2
Nick O'Leary	4-55	13.8	2
Christian Green	2-39	19.5	0
Devonta Freeman	3-35	11.7	0
Isaiah Jones	1-16	16.0	0
Karlos Williams	1-(15)	15.0	0
Shayne Broxsie	1-7	7.0	0
Total	26-431	16.6	5

Devonta Freeman scores Florida State's second touchdown against Maryland.

FLORIDA STATE 63 • MARYLAND 0

Kelvin Benjamin tries breaking a tackle. Benjamin had five receptions with two touchdowns against the Terrapins.

41

GAME 5 · OCT. 5, 2013

Nick O'Leary catches one of his two touchdown receptions.

FLORIDA STATE 63 · MARYLAND 0

Kenny Shaw had five catches and one touchdown against the Terps.

Jameis Winston picks up a few of his 24 rushing yards, but the freshman really damaged Maryland with his arm, completing 23 of 32 attempts for 393 yards and five touchdowns.

Rashad Greene hauls in one of his four catches for 108 yards.

GAME 6 • OCT. 19, 2013

FLORIDA STATE 51
CLEMSON 14

	1	2	3	4	F
Florida State	17	10	14	10	51
Clemson	7	0	0	7	14

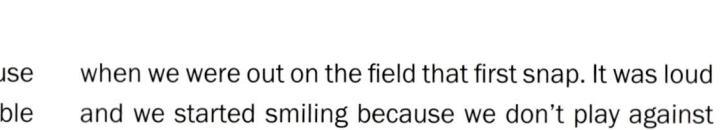

Death Valley is dead. Florida State's own house of horrors is no more, gone in one memorable night.

Losers of five consecutive games inside the unfriendly confines of Clemson's Memorial Stadium, the No. 5 'Noles buried the No. 3 Tigers 51-14 under their home turf in such a manner that had never been seen before. And the entire college football world watched it happen on ESPN in one sustained whistle-to-whistle triumphant performance.

In front of an orange-clad crowd of 83,428, the Seminoles played the role of silencer, quieting the rowdy masses with a forced fumble on the game's first play that would be turned into points. Things finished up with Jimbo Fisher and Jameis Winston victory interviews with ESPN's Chris Fowler.

In Death Valley's storied history, no team had ever scored more than 48 points against the Tigers. But the 'Noles hung 51 on Clemson and probably could have scored more. They were that dominant. Billed as the biggest ACC game in history, Florida State laid the biggest whooping on home-team Clemson ever.

Winston threw for 445 yards and three touchdowns to lead the rout, which put the Seminoles squarely in the hunt for a national championship. He completed 22 of 34 passes and rushed for a score to lead a 565-yard offensive effort. The 'Noles averaged 7.7 yards per play against the Tigers' defense.

"We don't play against noise. We're playing against the Clemson Tigers," said Winston. "It was amazing, when we were out on the field that first snap. It was loud and we started smiling because we don't play against noise."

"They're mature, they're growing, they're older, they understand the moments," said FSU head coach Jimbo Fisher of his team after the convincing victory over their ACC rivals.

Clemson took the opening kickoff, and on the first play from scrimmage, the Tigers' Stanton Seckinger fumbled after a 9-yard reception. Terrence Brooks recovered for FSU, and the 'Noles needed just three plays to go up 7-0 on a 22-yard touchdown pass from Winston to Kelvin Benjamin.

After Clemson managed to get just inside FSU territory on its next possession, the Seminoles went on a 16-play, 77-yard march that took 7:39 and ended with a 28-yard field goal by Roberto Aguayo for a 10-0 lead.

The Tigers turned the ball over again as quarterback Tajh Boyd was sacked by Lamarcus Joyner, and he fumbled. Mario Edwards scooped up the ball and raced 37 yards for a touchdown and a 17-0 lead with 3:07 left in the opening quarter.

Clemson recovered long enough to cut the deficit to 17-7 with less than a minute left in the quarter on a 3-yard pass by Boyd.

Midway through the second quarter, Winston struck again, this time on a 72-yard pass to Rashad Greene for a 24-7 FSU advantage. Another interception by the Florida State defense led to an Aguayo 24-yard field goal

Rashad Greene hauls in one of his four catches for 108 yards.

GAME 6 • OCT. 19, 2013

FLORIDA STATE 51
CLEMSON 14

	1	2	3	4	F
Florida State	17	10	14	10	51
Clemson	7	0	0	7	14

Death Valley is dead. Florida State's own house of horrors is no more, gone in one memorable night.

Losers of five consecutive games inside the unfriendly confines of Clemson's Memorial Stadium, the No. 5 'Noles buried the No. 3 Tigers 51-14 under their home turf in such a manner that had never been seen before. And the entire college football world watched it happen on ESPN in one sustained whistle-to-whistle triumphant performance.

In front of an orange-clad crowd of 83,428, the Seminoles played the role of silencer, quieting the rowdy masses with a forced fumble on the game's first play that would be turned into points. Things finished up with Jimbo Fisher and Jameis Winston victory interviews with ESPN's Chris Fowler.

In Death Valley's storied history, no team had ever scored more than 48 points against the Tigers. But the 'Noles hung 51 on Clemson and probably could have scored more. They were that dominant. Billed as the biggest ACC game in history, Florida State laid the biggest whooping on home-team Clemson ever.

Winston threw for 445 yards and three touchdowns to lead the rout, which put the Seminoles squarely in the hunt for a national championship. He completed 22 of 34 passes and rushed for a score to lead a 565-yard offensive effort. The 'Noles averaged 7.7 yards per play against the Tigers' defense.

"We don't play against noise. We're playing against the Clemson Tigers," said Winston. "It was amazing, when we were out on the field that first snap. It was loud and we started smiling because we don't play against noise."

"They're mature, they're growing, they're older, they understand the moments," said FSU head coach Jimbo Fisher of his team after the convincing victory over their ACC rivals.

Clemson took the opening kickoff, and on the first play from scrimmage, the Tigers' Stanton Seckinger fumbled after a 9-yard reception. Terrence Brooks recovered for FSU, and the 'Noles needed just three plays to go up 7-0 on a 22-yard touchdown pass from Winston to Kelvin Benjamin.

After Clemson managed to get just inside FSU territory on its next possession, the Seminoles went on a 16-play, 77-yard march that took 7:39 and ended with a 28-yard field goal by Roberto Aguayo for a 10-0 lead.

The Tigers turned the ball over again as quarterback Tajh Boyd was sacked by Lamarcus Joyner, and he fumbled. Mario Edwards scooped up the ball and raced 37 yards for a touchdown and a 17-0 lead with 3:07 left in the opening quarter.

Clemson recovered long enough to cut the deficit to 17-7 with less than a minute left in the quarter on a 3-yard pass by Boyd.

Midway through the second quarter, Winston struck again, this time on a 72-yard pass to Rashad Greene for a 24-7 FSU advantage. Another interception by the Florida State defense led to an Aguayo 24-yard field goal

Rashad Greene hauls in one of his four catches for 108 yards.

GAME 6 • OCT. 19, 2013

FLORIDA STATE 51
CLEMSON 14

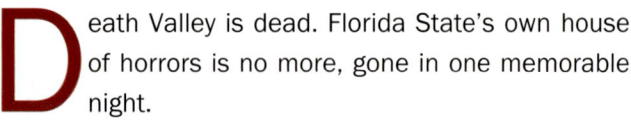

	1	2	3	4	F
Florida State	17	10	14	10	51
Clemson	7	0	0	7	14

Death Valley is dead. Florida State's own house of horrors is no more, gone in one memorable night.

Losers of five consecutive games inside the unfriendly confines of Clemson's Memorial Stadium, the No. 5 'Noles buried the No. 3 Tigers 51-14 under their home turf in such a manner that had never been seen before. And the entire college football world watched it happen on ESPN in one sustained whistle-to-whistle triumphant performance.

In front of an orange-clad crowd of 83,428, the Seminoles played the role of silencer, quieting the rowdy masses with a forced fumble on the game's first play that would be turned into points. Things finished up with Jimbo Fisher and Jameis Winston victory interviews with ESPN's Chris Fowler.

In Death Valley's storied history, no team had ever scored more than 48 points against the Tigers. But the 'Noles hung 51 on Clemson and probably could have scored more. They were that dominant. Billed as the biggest ACC game in history, Florida State laid the biggest whooping on home-team Clemson ever.

Winston threw for 445 yards and three touchdowns to lead the rout, which put the Seminoles squarely in the hunt for a national championship. He completed 22 of 34 passes and rushed for a score to lead a 565-yard offensive effort. The 'Noles averaged 7.7 yards per play against the Tigers' defense.

"We don't play against noise. We're playing against the Clemson Tigers," said Winston. "It was amazing, when we were out on the field that first snap. It was loud and we started smiling because we don't play against noise."

"They're mature, they're growing, they're older, they understand the moments," said FSU head coach Jimbo Fisher of his team after the convincing victory over their ACC rivals.

Clemson took the opening kickoff, and on the first play from scrimmage, the Tigers' Stanton Seckinger fumbled after a 9-yard reception. Terrence Brooks recovered for FSU, and the 'Noles needed just three plays to go up 7-0 on a 22-yard touchdown pass from Winston to Kelvin Benjamin.

After Clemson managed to get just inside FSU territory on its next possession, the Seminoles went on a 16-play, 77-yard march that took 7:39 and ended with a 28-yard field goal by Roberto Aguayo for a 10-0 lead.

The Tigers turned the ball over again as quarterback Tajh Boyd was sacked by Lamarcus Joyner, and he fumbled. Mario Edwards scooped up the ball and raced 37 yards for a touchdown and a 17-0 lead with 3:07 left in the opening quarter.

Clemson recovered long enough to cut the deficit to 17-7 with less than a minute left in the quarter on a 3-yard pass by Boyd.

Midway through the second quarter, Winston struck again, this time on a 72-yard pass to Rashad Greene for a 24-7 FSU advantage. Another interception by the Florida State defense led to an Aguayo 24-yard field goal

FLORIDA STATE 63 · MARYLAND 0

Rashad Greene hauls in one of his four catches for 108 yards.

GAME 6 • OCT. 19, 2013

FLORIDA STATE 51
CLEMSON 14

	1	2	3	4	F
Florida State	17	10	14	10	51
Clemson	7	0	0	7	14

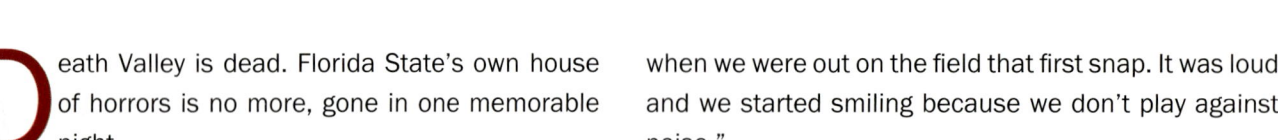

Death Valley is dead. Florida State's own house of horrors is no more, gone in one memorable night.

Losers of five consecutive games inside the unfriendly confines of Clemson's Memorial Stadium, the No. 5 'Noles buried the No. 3 Tigers 51-14 under their home turf in such a manner that had never been seen before. And the entire college football world watched it happen on ESPN in one sustained whistle-to-whistle triumphant performance.

In front of an orange-clad crowd of 83,428, the Seminoles played the role of silencer, quieting the rowdy masses with a forced fumble on the game's first play that would be turned into points. Things finished up with Jimbo Fisher and Jameis Winston victory interviews with ESPN's Chris Fowler.

In Death Valley's storied history, no team had ever scored more than 48 points against the Tigers. But the 'Noles hung 51 on Clemson and probably could have scored more. They were that dominant. Billed as the biggest ACC game in history, Florida State laid the biggest whooping on home-team Clemson ever.

Winston threw for 445 yards and three touchdowns to lead the rout, which put the Seminoles squarely in the hunt for a national championship. He completed 22 of 34 passes and rushed for a score to lead a 565-yard offensive effort. The 'Noles averaged 7.7 yards per play against the Tigers' defense.

"We don't play against noise. We're playing against the Clemson Tigers," said Winston. "It was amazing, when we were out on the field that first snap. It was loud and we started smiling because we don't play against noise."

"They're mature, they're growing, they're older, they understand the moments," said FSU head coach Jimbo Fisher of his team after the convincing victory over their ACC rivals.

Clemson took the opening kickoff, and on the first play from scrimmage, the Tigers' Stanton Seckinger fumbled after a 9-yard reception. Terrence Brooks recovered for FSU, and the 'Noles needed just three plays to go up 7-0 on a 22-yard touchdown pass from Winston to Kelvin Benjamin.

After Clemson managed to get just inside FSU territory on its next possession, the Seminoles went on a 16-play, 77-yard march that took 7:39 and ended with a 28-yard field goal by Roberto Aguayo for a 10-0 lead.

The Tigers turned the ball over again as quarterback Tajh Boyd was sacked by Lamarcus Joyner, and he fumbled. Mario Edwards scooped up the ball and raced 37 yards for a touchdown and a 17-0 lead with 3:07 left in the opening quarter.

Clemson recovered long enough to cut the deficit to 17-7 with less than a minute left in the quarter on a 3-yard pass by Boyd.

Midway through the second quarter, Winston struck again, this time on a 72-yard pass to Rashad Greene for a 24-7 FSU advantage. Another interception by the Florida State defense led to an Aguayo 24-yard field goal

FLORIDA STATE 63 · MARYLAND 0

Rashad Greene hauls in one of his four catches for 108 yards.

GAME 6 • OCT. 19, 2013

FLORIDA STATE 51
CLEMSON 14

	1	2	3	4	F
Florida State	17	10	14	10	51
Clemson	7	0	0	7	14

Death Valley is dead. Florida State's own house of horrors is no more, gone in one memorable night.

Losers of five consecutive games inside the unfriendly confines of Clemson's Memorial Stadium, the No. 5 'Noles buried the No. 3 Tigers 51-14 under their home turf in such a manner that had never been seen before. And the entire college football world watched it happen on ESPN in one sustained whistle-to-whistle triumphant performance.

In front of an orange-clad crowd of 83,428, the Seminoles played the role of silencer, quieting the rowdy masses with a forced fumble on the game's first play that would be turned into points. Things finished up with Jimbo Fisher and Jameis Winston victory interviews with ESPN's Chris Fowler.

In Death Valley's storied history, no team had ever scored more than 48 points against the Tigers. But the 'Noles hung 51 on Clemson and probably could have scored more. They were that dominant. Billed as the biggest ACC game in history, Florida State laid the biggest whooping on home-team Clemson ever.

Winston threw for 445 yards and three touchdowns to lead the rout, which put the Seminoles squarely in the hunt for a national championship. He completed 22 of 34 passes and rushed for a score to lead a 565-yard offensive effort. The 'Noles averaged 7.7 yards per play against the Tigers' defense.

"We don't play against noise. We're playing against the Clemson Tigers," said Winston. "It was amazing, when we were out on the field that first snap. It was loud and we started smiling because we don't play against noise."

"They're mature, they're growing, they're older, they understand the moments," said FSU head coach Jimbo Fisher of his team after the convincing victory over their ACC rivals.

Clemson took the opening kickoff, and on the first play from scrimmage, the Tigers' Stanton Seckinger fumbled after a 9-yard reception. Terrence Brooks recovered for FSU, and the 'Noles needed just three plays to go up 7-0 on a 22-yard touchdown pass from Winston to Kelvin Benjamin.

After Clemson managed to get just inside FSU territory on its next possession, the Seminoles went on a 16-play, 77-yard march that took 7:39 and ended with a 28-yard field goal by Roberto Aguayo for a 10-0 lead.

The Tigers turned the ball over again as quarterback Tajh Boyd was sacked by Lamarcus Joyner, and he fumbled. Mario Edwards scooped up the ball and raced 37 yards for a touchdown and a 17-0 lead with 3:07 left in the opening quarter.

Clemson recovered long enough to cut the deficit to 17-7 with less than a minute left in the quarter on a 3-yard pass by Boyd.

Midway through the second quarter, Winston struck again, this time on a 72-yard pass to Rashad Greene for a 24-7 FSU advantage. Another interception by the Florida State defense led to an Aguayo 24-yard field goal

Rashad Greene hauls in one of his four catches for 108 yards.

GAME 6 • OCT. 19, 2013

FLORIDA STATE 51
CLEMSON 14

	1	2	3	4	F
Florida State	17	10	14	10	51
Clemson	7	0	0	7	14

Death Valley is dead. Florida State's own house of horrors is no more, gone in one memorable night.

Losers of five consecutive games inside the unfriendly confines of Clemson's Memorial Stadium, the No. 5 'Noles buried the No. 3 Tigers 51-14 under their home turf in such a manner that had never been seen before. And the entire college football world watched it happen on ESPN in one sustained whistle-to-whistle triumphant performance.

In front of an orange-clad crowd of 83,428, the Seminoles played the role of silencer, quieting the rowdy masses with a forced fumble on the game's first play that would be turned into points. Things finished up with Jimbo Fisher and Jameis Winston victory interviews with ESPN's Chris Fowler.

In Death Valley's storied history, no team had ever scored more than 48 points against the Tigers. But the 'Noles hung 51 on Clemson and probably could have scored more. They were that dominant. Billed as the biggest ACC game in history, Florida State laid the biggest whooping on home-team Clemson ever.

Winston threw for 445 yards and three touchdowns to lead the rout, which put the Seminoles squarely in the hunt for a national championship. He completed 22 of 34 passes and rushed for a score to lead a 565-yard offensive effort. The 'Noles averaged 7.7 yards per play against the Tigers' defense.

"We don't play against noise. We're playing against the Clemson Tigers," said Winston. "It was amazing, when we were out on the field that first snap. It was loud and we started smiling because we don't play against noise."

"They're mature, they're growing, they're older, they understand the moments," said FSU head coach Jimbo Fisher of his team after the convincing victory over their ACC rivals.

Clemson took the opening kickoff, and on the first play from scrimmage, the Tigers' Stanton Seckinger fumbled after a 9-yard reception. Terrence Brooks recovered for FSU, and the 'Noles needed just three plays to go up 7-0 on a 22-yard touchdown pass from Winston to Kelvin Benjamin.

After Clemson managed to get just inside FSU territory on its next possession, the Seminoles went on a 16-play, 77-yard march that took 7:39 and ended with a 28-yard field goal by Roberto Aguayo for a 10-0 lead.

The Tigers turned the ball over again as quarterback Tajh Boyd was sacked by Lamarcus Joyner, and he fumbled. Mario Edwards scooped up the ball and raced 37 yards for a touchdown and a 17-0 lead with 3:07 left in the opening quarter.

Clemson recovered long enough to cut the deficit to 17-7 with less than a minute left in the quarter on a 3-yard pass by Boyd.

Midway through the second quarter, Winston struck again, this time on a 72-yard pass to Rashad Greene for a 24-7 FSU advantage. Another interception by the Florida State defense led to an Aguayo 24-yard field goal

Rashad Greene hauls in one of his four catches for 108 yards.

GAME 6 • OCT. 19, 2013
FLORIDA STATE 51
CLEMSON 14

	1	2	3	4	F
Florida State	17	10	14	10	51
Clemson	7	0	0	7	14

Death Valley is dead. Florida State's own house of horrors is no more, gone in one memorable night.

Losers of five consecutive games inside the unfriendly confines of Clemson's Memorial Stadium, the No. 5 'Noles buried the No. 3 Tigers 51-14 under their home turf in such a manner that had never been seen before. And the entire college football world watched it happen on ESPN in one sustained whistle-to-whistle triumphant performance.

In front of an orange-clad crowd of 83,428, the Seminoles played the role of silencer, quieting the rowdy masses with a forced fumble on the game's first play that would be turned into points. Things finished up with Jimbo Fisher and Jameis Winston victory interviews with ESPN's Chris Fowler.

In Death Valley's storied history, no team had ever scored more than 48 points against the Tigers. But the 'Noles hung 51 on Clemson and probably could have scored more. They were that dominant. Billed as the biggest ACC game in history, Florida State laid the biggest whooping on home-team Clemson ever.

Winston threw for 445 yards and three touchdowns to lead the rout, which put the Seminoles squarely in the hunt for a national championship. He completed 22 of 34 passes and rushed for a score to lead a 565-yard offensive effort. The 'Noles averaged 7.7 yards per play against the Tigers' defense.

"We don't play against noise. We're playing against the Clemson Tigers," said Winston. "It was amazing, when we were out on the field that first snap. It was loud and we started smiling because we don't play against noise."

"They're mature, they're growing, they're older, they understand the moments," said FSU head coach Jimbo Fisher of his team after the convincing victory over their ACC rivals.

Clemson took the opening kickoff, and on the first play from scrimmage, the Tigers' Stanton Seckinger fumbled after a 9-yard reception. Terrence Brooks recovered for FSU, and the 'Noles needed just three plays to go up 7-0 on a 22-yard touchdown pass from Winston to Kelvin Benjamin.

After Clemson managed to get just inside FSU territory on its next possession, the Seminoles went on a 16-play, 77-yard march that took 7:39 and ended with a 28-yard field goal by Roberto Aguayo for a 10-0 lead.

The Tigers turned the ball over again as quarterback Tajh Boyd was sacked by Lamarcus Joyner, and he fumbled. Mario Edwards scooped up the ball and raced 37 yards for a touchdown and a 17-0 lead with 3:07 left in the opening quarter.

Clemson recovered long enough to cut the deficit to 17-7 with less than a minute left in the quarter on a 3-yard pass by Boyd.

Midway through the second quarter, Winston struck again, this time on a 72-yard pass to Rashad Greene for a 24-7 FSU advantage. Another interception by the Florida State defense led to an Aguayo 24-yard field goal

just before the half as the 'Noles padded their lead to 27-7.

In the third quarter, Winston threw his third scoring pass on FSU's first drive, a 17-yard strike to Greene, and later, Winston added a 4-yard scamper as the 'Noles were firmly in control at 41-7.

Devonta Freeman had a 2-yard run early in the fourth quarter, and Aguayo added his third field goal as the Seminoles completed the stunning victory. The Tigers got a late touchdown from backup quarterback Cole Stoudt in the final seconds.

Greene led the 'Noles with eight catches for 146 yards and two touchdowns. Nick O'Leary added five catches for 161 yards. Freeman rushed 21 times for 84 yards and one score.

The Florida State defense forced four Clemson turnovers, and the Seminoles scored 24 points off the Tiger miscues. Joyner had eight tackles and a sack, and he accounted for all three FSU takeaways in the first half with an interception and two forced fumbles. Telvin Smith led the FSU defense in total tackles with 11.

Boyd was 17 of 37 passing for 156 yards and two interceptions for Clemson, which had 326 total yards and 3.8 yards per play on offense. Boyd was also sacked four times by the aggressive 'Noles defense.

SCORING SUMMARY

First Quarter
FSU	13:38	TD	Benjamin 22-yd pass (Aguayo kick)
FSU	4:18	FG	Aguayo 28-yd
FSU	3:07	TD	Edwards 37-yd fumble rec (Aguayo kick)
CU	:51	TD	Watkins 3-yd pass (Catanzaro kick)

Second Quarter
| FSU | 7:08 | TD | Greene 72-yd pass (Aguayo kick) |
| FSU | :03 | FG | Aguayo 24-yd |

Third Quarter
| FSU | 13:33 | TD | Greene 17-yd pass (Aguayo kick) |
| FSU | 4:04 | TD | Winston 4-yd rush (Aguayo kick) |

Fourth Quarter
FSU	12:17	TD	Freeman 2-yd rush (Aguayo kick)
FSU	4:41	FG	Aguayo 20-yd
CU	:13	TD	Stoudt 2-yd rush (Catanzaro kick)

FLORIDA STATE STATS

Passing
Name	Comp-Att-Int	Yards	TD
Jameis Winston	22-34-1	445	3
TEAM	0-1-0	0	0
Total	22-35-1	445	3

Rushing
Name	Att-Yards	Avg	TD
Devonta Freeman	21-84	4.0	1
Karlos Williams	3-19	6.3	0
James Wilder Jr.	5-12	2.4	0
Chad Abram	1-3	3.0	0
Jameis Winston	7-2	0.3	1
Christian Green	1-1	1.0	0
Total	38-121	3.2	2

Receiving
Name	Att-Yards	Avg	TD
Nick O'Leary	5-161	32.2	0
Rashad Greene	8-146	18.3	2
Kenny Shaw	5-64	12.8	0
Kelvin Benjamin	3-62	20.7	1
Devonta Freeman	1-11	11.0	0
Total	22-444	20.2	3

GAME 6 · OCT. 19, 2013

Mario Edwards Jr. takes off with a Tajh Boyd fumble forced by Lamarcus Joyner in the first quarter. Edwards returned it 37 yards for a touchdown to give the Seminoles a 17-0 lead.

Jameis Winston calls out the signals against Clemson. Winston led the Seminoles to 565 offensive yards, completing 22 of 34 pass attempts for 445 yards and three touchdowns, while rushing for one score.

Kelvin Benjamin uses his 6-foot-5 frame to haul in this reception against the Tigers.

Defensive tackle Timmy Jernigan tries to get a second arm around Clemson quarterback Tajh Boyd. The FSU defense forced four Clemson turnovers that resulted in 24 points, and sacked Boyd four times.

Devonta Freeman rushed for 84 yards and one touchdown in Death Valley.

Linebacker Christian Jones sacks Tajh Boyd.

James Wilder Jr. finds a big hole in the Clemson defense.

GAME 7 • OCT. 26, 2013

FLORIDA STATE 49
NORTH CAROLINA STATE 17

	1	2	3	4	F
North Carolina State	0	0	10	7	17
Florida State	35	7	0	7	49

Bobby Bowden planted Osceola's spear, and then major college football's all-time winningest coach watched his former team bury North Carolina State 49-17.

In a performance reminiscent of Florida State football's glory years when Bowden's teams were the best in the country — steamrolling lesser opponents and competing for national championships — coach Jimbo Fisher's No. 2 'Noles dropped 35 points on the Wolfpack in the first quarter before moving to 7-0 overall and 5-0 in the ACC.

"The emotions of coming off a big win at Clemson, I was very proud that we are learning to handle that better," said Fisher. "I thought we prepared well all week."

The last time FSU started a season 7-0 was 1999 when the Bowden-led 'Noles would eventually win the national title.

The Seminoles' first-team defense only played in the first half, and star quarterback Jameis Winston and the first-team offense only played the first series of the second half before calling it a day. N.C. State scored all 17 of its points against the 'Noles' second- and third-string players. Not counting the points that FSU's backups allowed, the Seminoles dismantled Maryland, Clemson and N.C. State by a combined score of 156-14 in 10 consecutive quarters.

"After coming off a big win, the main thing is you've got to keep that same kind of focus," said FSU senior cornerback Lamarcus Joyner. "Just keeping that focus is critical, and I was proud of how we did that. We weren't looking ahead, and we weren't looking back."

Winston's numbers weren't as eye-popping as they were the previous week at Clemson, but the Heisman Trophy candidate did add three more touchdown tosses to his 2013 totals in the win. Winston finished the day 16 of 26 passing for 292 yards, the trio of scores and one interception that bounced off Kelvin Benjamin's hands on the final first-team offensive drive.

Rashad Greene was Winston's favorite target, hauling in eight catches for 137 yards and one touchdown. Benjamin added three catches for 69 yards and a score, while Nick O'Leary also found the end zone. Devonta Freeman ran 12 times for 92 yards with two touchdowns, Karlos Williams had 13 runs for 86 yards and Kermit Whitfield took a reverse 33 yards for late a fourth-quarter score.

FSU racked up 550 yards of total offense and tied the school record for most points scored in a single quarter with 35 in the game's opening frame.

"These last two weeks we have just started off fast," said Winston. "If you get early turnovers and you get good field position, that's what happens when you have an offense like ours."

Just as they did against Clemson, the 'Noles forced a turnover on the game's first drive when Terrence Brooks hauled in a diving interception off Wolfpack quarterback Brandon Mitchell. Brooks later added a forced fumble. Ronald Darby also added an interception.

FSU's top four tacklers were all linebackers, with true freshman E.J. Levenberry posting a team-best eight stops. Reggie Northrup and Telvin Smith each had six tackles, and Terrance Smith had five tackles and a sack. Christian Jones also had a sack while matching DeMarcus Walker, Jacobbi McDaniel, Joyner, Marquez White and Nate Andrews with four tackles.

The Seminoles' defense didn't allow N.C. State to cross midfield until early in the second quarter, and the first-team defense allowed just 80 first-half yards. The Wolfpack finished the game with 316 total yards as Mitchell finished 17 of 33 passing for 128 yards.

"I feel like what our coaches harped on the most in this game was not settling," said Brooks. "Don't look at the scoreboard, just go out there and play every play."

SCORING SUMMARY

First Quarter
FS	13:02	TD	Williams 18-yd rush (Aguayo kick)
FS	11:12	TD	Benjamin 39-yd pass (Aguayo kick)
FS	7:02	TD	Freeman 11-yd rush (Aguayo kick)
FS	6:09	TD	O'Leary 14-yd pass (Aguayo kick)
FS	2:02	TD	Greene 42-yd pass (Aguayo kick)

Second Quarter
| FS | 3:06 | TD | Freeman 4-yd rush (Aguayo kick) |

Third Quarter
| NCS | 7:51 | FG | Sade 36-yd |
| NCS | :59 | TD | Thornton 72-yd rush (Sade kick) |

Fourth Quarter
| NCS | 7:16 | TD | Thornton 1-yd rush (Sade kick) |
| FS | 2:19 | TD | Whitfield 33-yd rush (Aguayo kick) |

FLORIDA STATE STATS

Passing

Name	Comp-Att-Int	Yards	TD
Jameis Winston	16-26-1	292	3
Jacob Coker	4-8-1	50	0
Total	20-34-2	342	3

Rushing

Name	Att-Yards	Avg	TD
Devonta Freeman	12-92	7.7	2
Karlos Williams	13-86	6.6	1
Kermit Whitfield	1-33	31.0	1
Ryan Green	2-19	9.5	0
Jacob Coker	5-7	1.4	0
Jameis Winston	1-(-11)	-11.0	0
Total	34-224	6.6	4

Receiving

Name	Att-Yards	Avg	TD
Rashad Greene	8-137	17.1	1
Kelvin Benjamin	3-69	23.0	1
Kenny Shaw	3-44	14.7	0
Devonta Freeman	1-30	30.0	0
Christian Green	2-22	11.0	0
Kermit Whitfield	1-16	16.0	0
Nick O'Leary	1-14	14.0	1
Karlos Williams	1-10	10.0	0
Total	20-342	17.1	3

Former head coach Bobby Bowden was honored prior to the kickoff against North Carolina State.

Devonta Freeman runs for some of his 92 rushing yards, and two touchdowns, against the Wolfpack. Freeman also caught one pass for 30 yards.

Defensive back Lamarcus Joyner puts a big hit on N.C. State running back Shadrach Thornton.

FLORIDA STATE 49 · N.C. STATE 17

FSU's first-team defense didn't let the Wolfpack cross midfield until the second quarter, and allowed only 80 first-half yards.

GAME 7 · OCT. 26, 2013

Jameis Winston led the Seminoles to a 42-0 halftime lead, including three touchdown passes.

Defensive end Dan Hicks tries to overpower N.C. State tight end Asa Watson.

GAME 8 • NOV. 2, 2013

FLORIDA STATE 41
MIAMI 14

	1	2	3	4	F
Miami	7	7	0	0	14
Florida State	7	14	14	6	41

The biggest crowd in Doak Campbell Stadium history saw more than just another statement win for the No. 3 Seminoles.

All 84,409 of the fans who packed into the house after a long day that started with ESPN's early-morning "College GameDay" broadcast and concluded with a late-night 41-14 mauling of the No. 7 Hurricanes were witnesses to a perfect example of what Jimbo Fisher has built since taking over as FSU's head coach prior to the 2010 season.

"This is a very good football team," said Fisher. "That's a very good football team that we just played and beating them by four touchdowns, that doesn't happen very often. Again, I say this, I love our football team. I love our football team."

'Noles opponents surely don't feel the same way. FSU scored 40 points in a school-record eight consecutive games and outscored ranked opponents 155-28. Credit the all-star roster that Fisher has put together.

The Seminoles clung to a 21-14 halftime advantage, and then the defense pinned its ears back and held the 'Canes scoreless in the final two frames. A quick scan of the personnel on that side of the ball makes it clear that the ingredients make up the winning recipe.

From Lamarcus Joyner to Jalen Ramsey to Telvin Smith and Christian Jones to Timmy Jernigan and Mario Edwards Jr. and on and on and on, four years of successful recruiting has stacked the defensive cupboard despite the loss of several NFL-bound 'Noles defenders.

Under Jeremy Pruitt — a rookie defensive coordinator hired by Fisher because of his championship pedigree and proven success as an assistant — the Seminoles transitioned from Mark Stoops' 4-3 scheme to a 3-4 before evolving midseason into a ferocious 3-3-5 that physically and mentally punished opponents.

"We are doing some pretty good things around here," said Joyner. "I see a chemistry and a continuity around here that may not be broken. We started from spring when we knew that it's us against the country. We built a standard and a belief and brotherhood around here that cannot be broken."

Even on a night when quarterback Jameis Winston wasn't his best, the redshirt freshman still threw for 325 yards and orchestrated an offense that outgained the 'Canes 517-275. Winston finished 21 of 29 passing, but was intercepted twice.

And the weapons at his disposal are aplenty.

Miami native Devonta Freeman took it to his hometown team with a memorable performance that saw him register 98 yards receiving and 78 yards rushing while totaling three touchdowns. He opened the scoring with a 5-yard run in the first quarter. His 48-yard touchdown reception in the second quarter marked the first of his career through the air, and his 12-yard touchdown run in the third quarter pushed the Seminoles' lead to 35-14.

Including Freeman, Winston's offense also features a host of future NFL draft selections in Nick O'Leary, James Wilder Jr., Karlos Wiliams, Rashad Greene, Kel-

FLORIDA STATE 49 · N.C. STATE 17

Defensive end Dan Hicks tries to overpower N.C. State tight end Asa Watson.

GAME 8 • NOV. 2, 2013
FLORIDA STATE 41
MIAMI 14

	1	2	3	4	F
Miami	7	7	0	0	14
Florida State	7	14	14	6	41

The biggest crowd in Doak Campbell Stadium history saw more than just another statement win for the No. 3 Seminoles.

All 84,409 of the fans who packed into the house after a long day that started with ESPN's early-morning "College GameDay" broadcast and concluded with a late-night 41-14 mauling of the No. 7 Hurricanes were witnesses to a perfect example of what Jimbo Fisher has built since taking over as FSU's head coach prior to the 2010 season.

"This is a very good football team," said Fisher. "That's a very good football team that we just played and beating them by four touchdowns, that doesn't happen very often. Again, I say this, I love our football team. I love our football team."

'Noles opponents surely don't feel the same way. FSU scored 40 points in a school-record eight consecutive games and outscored ranked opponents 155-28. Credit the all-star roster that Fisher has put together.

The Seminoles clung to a 21-14 halftime advantage, and then the defense pinned its ears back and held the 'Canes scoreless in the final two frames. A quick scan of the personnel on that side of the ball makes it clear that the ingredients make up the winning recipe.

From Lamarcus Joyner to Jalen Ramsey to Telvin Smith and Christian Jones to Timmy Jernigan and Mario Edwards Jr. and on and on and on, four years of successful recruiting has stacked the defensive cupboard despite the loss of several NFL-bound 'Noles defenders.

Under Jeremy Pruitt — a rookie defensive coordinator hired by Fisher because of his championship pedigree and proven success as an assistant — the Seminoles transitioned from Mark Stoops' 4-3 scheme to a 3-4 before evolving midseason into a ferocious 3-3-5 that physically and mentally punished opponents.

"We are doing some pretty good things around here," said Joyner. "I see a chemistry and a continuity around here that may not be broken. We started from spring when we knew that it's us against the country. We built a standard and a belief and brotherhood around here that cannot be broken."

Even on a night when quarterback Jameis Winston wasn't his best, the redshirt freshman still threw for 325 yards and orchestrated an offense that outgained the 'Canes 517-275. Winston finished 21 of 29 passing, but was intercepted twice.

And the weapons at his disposal are aplenty.

Miami native Devonta Freeman took it to his hometown team with a memorable performance that saw him register 98 yards receiving and 78 yards rushing while totaling three touchdowns. He opened the scoring with a 5-yard run in the first quarter. His 48-yard touchdown reception in the second quarter marked the first of his career through the air, and his 12-yard touchdown run in the third quarter pushed the Seminoles' lead to 35-14.

Including Freeman, Winston's offense also features a host of future NFL draft selections in Nick O'Leary, James Wilder Jr., Karlos Wiliams, Rashad Greene, Kel-

FLORIDA STATE 49 · N.C. STATE 17

Defensive end Dan Hicks tries to overpower N.C. State tight end Asa Watson.

GAME 8 • NOV. 2, 2013

FLORIDA STATE 41
MIAMI 14

	1	2	3	4	F
Miami	7	7	0	0	14
Florida State	7	14	14	6	41

The biggest crowd in Doak Campbell Stadium history saw more than just another statement win for the No. 3 Seminoles.

All 84,409 of the fans who packed into the house after a long day that started with ESPN's early-morning "College GameDay" broadcast and concluded with a late-night 41-14 mauling of the No. 7 Hurricanes were witnesses to a perfect example of what Jimbo Fisher has built since taking over as FSU's head coach prior to the 2010 season.

"This is a very good football team," said Fisher. "That's a very good football team that we just played and beating them by four touchdowns, that doesn't happen very often. Again, I say this, I love our football team. I love our football team."

'Noles opponents surely don't feel the same way. FSU scored 40 points in a school-record eight consecutive games and outscored ranked opponents 155-28. Credit the all-star roster that Fisher has put together.

The Seminoles clung to a 21-14 halftime advantage, and then the defense pinned its ears back and held the 'Canes scoreless in the final two frames. A quick scan of the personnel on that side of the ball makes it clear that the ingredients make up the winning recipe.

From Lamarcus Joyner to Jalen Ramsey to Telvin Smith and Christian Jones to Timmy Jernigan and Mario Edwards Jr. and on and on and on, four years of successful recruiting has stacked the defensive cupboard despite the loss of several NFL-bound 'Noles defenders.

Under Jeremy Pruitt — a rookie defensive coordinator hired by Fisher because of his championship pedigree and proven success as an assistant — the Seminoles transitioned from Mark Stoops' 4-3 scheme to a 3-4 before evolving midseason into a ferocious 3-3-5 that physically and mentally punished opponents.

"We are doing some pretty good things around here," said Joyner. "I see a chemistry and a continuity around here that may not be broken. We started from spring when we knew that it's us against the country. We built a standard and a belief and brotherhood around here that cannot be broken."

Even on a night when quarterback Jameis Winston wasn't his best, the redshirt freshman still threw for 325 yards and orchestrated an offense that outgained the 'Canes 517-275. Winston finished 21 of 29 passing, but was intercepted twice.

And the weapons at his disposal are aplenty.

Miami native Devonta Freeman took it to his hometown team with a memorable performance that saw him register 98 yards receiving and 78 yards rushing while totaling three touchdowns. He opened the scoring with a 5-yard run in the first quarter. His 48-yard touchdown reception in the second quarter marked the first of his career through the air, and his 12-yard touchdown run in the third quarter pushed the Seminoles' lead to 35-14.

Including Freeman, Winston's offense also features a host of future NFL draft selections in Nick O'Leary, James Wilder Jr., Karlos Wiliams, Rashad Greene, Kel-

vin Benjamin and Kenny Shaw, as well as an offensive line that may be the country's best.

Wilder scored twice on a 5-yard run with 8:33 remaining in the third quarter to push FSU's lead to 28-14 and a 1-yard first-half rush.

FSU finished the game 11 of 15 on third-down conversions and consistently kept Miami backpedaling. The 'Noles depth, playmaking ability and sustained success make it virtually impossible for a defense to derail.

It's toughness and grit — like that showed by the defense — also played a role, again. Playing big, playing fast and playing physical has always been Fisher's No. 1 goal, and with this 2013 team he has those traits all rolled into one seemingly unstoppable squad.

"Just because you're physical, doesn't mean you're not skilled," said Fisher. "Just because you're skilled, doesn't mean you're not physical. That's the way we want to be. I want to be the most physically dominating team that has great skill.

"When you have a good football team, that's the way you play football."

SCORING SUMMARY

First Quarter
| FS | 9:16 | TD | Freeman 5-yd rush (Aguayo kick) |
| UM | 2:43 | TD | Hurns 33-yd pass (Goudis kick) |

Second Quarter
FS	10:42	TD	Wilder 1-yd rush (Aguayo kick)
FS	5:08	TD	Freeman 48-yd pass (Aguayo kick)
UM	:22	TD	Hurns 14-yd pass (Goudis kick)

Third Quarter
| FS | 8:33 | TD | Wilder 5-yd rush (Aguayo kick) |
| FS | 3:41 | TD | Freeman 12-yd rush (Aguayo kick) |

Fourth Quarter
| FS | 6:52 | FG | Aguayo 25-yd |
| FS | 1:03 | FG | Aguayo 28-yd |

FLORIDA STATE STATS

Passing

Name	Comp-Att-Int	Yards	TD
Jameis Winston	21-29-2	325	1
Total	21-29-2	325	1

Rushing

Name	Att-Yards	Avg	TD
Devonta Freeman	23-78	3.4	2
Karlos Williams	5-46	9.2	0
James Wilder Jr.	9-42	4.7	2
Jameis Winston	6-27	4.5	0
TEAM	1-(-1)	-1.0	0
Total	44-192	4.4	4

Receiving

Name	Att-Yards	Avg	TD
Devonta Freeman	6-98	16.3	1
Rashad Greene	6-83	13.8	0
Kelvin Benjamin	2-46	23.0	0
Nick O'Leary	3-45	15.0	0
Kenny Shaw	3-(44)	14.7	0
Chad Abram	1-9	9.0	0
Total	21-325	15.5	1

Devonta Freeman tries to break free from a Miami defender.

James Wilder Jr. dives for one of his two touchdowns against the Hurricanes.

Kelvin Benjamin goes high to catch a pass.

Christian Jones (7) and Timmy Jernigan (8) bring down Miami running back Duke Johnson.

Devonta Freeman led the Seminoles with 78 yards rushing and two touchdowns, and he also caught six passes for 98 yards and one touchdown.

FLORIDA STATE 41 · MIAMI 14

P.J. Williams steps in front of a Miami receiver for an interception in the 41-14 victory.

GAME 9 • NOV. 9, 2013

FLORIDA STATE 59
WAKE FOREST 3

	1	2	3	4	F
Florida State	21	21	10	7	59
Wake Forest	0	0	0	3	3

How did No. 2 Florida State respond after being handed control of its own national-championship destiny? Its defense delivered an ACC Atlantic Division title at Wake Forest.

In a 59-3 walloping of Wake at BB&T Field, the 9-0 Seminoles used a dominating defense to at least guarantee itself a trip to Charlotte and the chance to defend its conference crown.

The Seminoles were so good defensively against the Demon Deacons that Heisman Trophy hopeful Jameis Winston and his high-powered offense were merely an afterthought in the drubbing. From a statistical standpoint, the victory won't turn any heads — Winston threw for a career-low 159 yards in a little more than two quarters of play (but he did set the ACC freshman record for passing touchdowns in a season with his 25th and 26th of the year in only nine games) and the 'Noles generated a season-low 296 total yards — but the team did extend the school record of consecutive games scoring at least 40 points to nine.

The offense didn't have to be its usual special self. Instead, the defense, which rested its starters after the first drive of the second half but still forced seven total turnovers, was spectacular enough to carry the victory.

FSU tied a school record in the blowout with six interceptions. The Seminoles had 107 interception return yards with one score while Wake Forest only had 166 total yards of offense.

Starting in place of injured starter Terrence Brooks, rookie Nate Andrews shone brightest in a star-studded defensive showing. Andrews finished with two interceptions — one of which he took back 56 yards for FSU's first defensive score — and then forced a fumble that was scooped up and scored with by fellow freshman Jalen Ramsey that gave the Seminoles a 35-0 second-quarter lead.

"Nate has been surprising us and he's been doing a good job so far," said FSU senior linebacker Christian Jones. "We are looking forward to seeing him keep improving; he's a good player. He had a big game. He capitalized on this opportunity."

He wasn't the only one to make an impact.

Jones also had a hand in the turnover party, smashing Wake Forest quarterback Tanner Price in the first quarter and forcing an errant pass that was intercepted by Mario Edwards Jr.

Jones then intercepted Demon Deacons backup quarterback Tyler Cameron on the first and only play the first-team defense would play in the second half.

Edwards' interception gave FSU the ball on Wake Forest's 27-yard line, which two plays later resulted in an 18-yard Kelvin Benjamin score that padded the 'Noles' lead at 21-0 after two Devonta Freeman and James Wilder Jr. scoring runs put the visitors on top for good earlier. Jones' interception gave FSU the ball at the Wake Forest 5-yard line and was immediately followed by a short Karlos Williams touchdown run that extended the Seminoles' advantage to 49-0.

Terrance Smith and Marquez White both had interceptions as well. Collectively, Wake Forest's three quar-

terbacks who played had nearly as many interceptions (six) as completions (seven).

"That's something we always talk about doing is getting a lot of turnovers," said Jones. "It worked out in our favor today."

Reggie Northrup led the way with eight tackles and a half tackle for loss for the Atlantic Division champs. Timmy Jernigan and E.J. Levenberry both had six stops, and Demonte McAllister and Lamarcus Joyner had four tackles apiece.

FSU limited the Demon Deacons to 2.6 yards per play and just five third-down conversions on 17 attempts.

Offensively, Greene hauled in five of Winston's passes for 47 yards while Nick O'Leary and Karlos Williams each had three grabs. One of Williams' catches came from Jacob Coker, who replaced Winston early in the third quarter. Chad Abram caught Winston's second touchdown toss.

Freshman wide receiver Kermit Whitfield didn't get involved in the offense but that didn't stop him from updating the scoreboard. His 97-yard special-teams touchdown in the fourth quarter was Florida State's first kick return score since 2008.

With the victory, Florida State clinched its third Atlantic Division title in four years under head coach Jimbo Fisher. But bigger and better things were just down the road.

SCORING SUMMARY

First Quarter
FS	7:15	TD	Wilder 5-yd rush (Aguayo kick)
FS	6:25	TD	Freeman 1-yd rush (Aguayo kick)
FS	2:10	TD	Benjamin 18-yd pass (Aguayo kick)

Second Quarter
FS	14:15	TD	Andrews 56-yd INT (Aguayo kick)
FS	13:56	TD	Ramsey 23-yd fumble rec (Aguayo kick)
FS	:11	TD	Abram 2-yd pass (Aguayo kick)

Third Quarter
FS	12:03	TD	Williams 5-yd rush (Aguayo kick)
FS	8:24	FG	Aguayo 42-yd

Fourth Quarter
WF	9:07	FG	Hedlund 23-yd
FS	8:52	TD	Whitfield 97-yd KO ret (Aguayo kick)

FLORIDA STATE STATS

Passing
Name	Comp-Att-Int	Yards	TD
Jameis Winston	17-28-1	159	2
Jacob Coker	4-9-0	37	0
Sean Maguire	1-2-0	11	0
Total	22-39-1	207	2

Rushing
Name	Att-Yards	Avg	TD
James Wilder Jr.	6-49	8.2	1
Karlos Williams	12-49	4.1	1
Devonta Freeman	6-11	1.8	1
Rashad Greene	1-9	9.0	0
Jameis Winston	3-4	1.3	0
Ryan Green	3-(-2)	-0.7	0
Sean Maguire	1-(-7)	-7.0	0
Jacob Coker	2-(-24)	-12.0	0
Total	34-89	2.6	3

Receiving
Name	Att-Yards	Avg	TD
Rashad Greene	5-47	9.4	0
Nick O'Leary	3-37	12.3	0
Christian Green	2-24	12.0	0
Kelvin Benjamin	2-23	11.5	1
Karlos Williams	3-21	7.0	0
Chad Abram	2-18	9.0	1
Shayne Broxsie	1-12	12.0	0
Jesus Wilson	1-11	11.0	0
Christian Jones	1-11	11.0	0
Kenny Shaw	1-4	4.0	0
Devonta Freeman	1-(-1)	-1.0	0
Total	22-207	9.4	2

GAME 9 • NOV. 9, 2013

■ Christian Jones had a big game against Wake Forest, sacking quarterback Tanner Price in the first quarter and forcing an errant pass that was intercepted by Mario Edwards Jr. On the first play of the second half, Jones had an interception, and then the FSU first-team defense was given the rest of the day off.

Karlos Williams squeezes through a hole in the Wake Forest defense.

GAME 9 • NOV. 9, 2013

■ Christian Green tries to break free against the Demon Deacons.

■ Thanks to the FSU defense, Jameis Winston had a "quiet" day, completing 17 of 28 for 159 yards and two touchdowns.

FLORIDA STATE 59 · WAKE FOREST 3

Lamarcus Joyner lowers the boom while Terrance Smith zeroes in on the ball carrier.

With the victory over Wake Forest, FSU clinched its third Atlantic Division title in four years under head coach Jimbo Fisher.

FLORIDA STATE 59 · WAKE FOREST 3

Kelvin Benjamin celebrates his 18-yard touchdown reception with an offensive lineman.

GAME 10 • NOV. 16, 2013

FLORIDA STATE 59
SYRACUSE 3

	1	2	3	4	F
Syracuse	0	0	0	3	3
Florida State	28	10	21	0	59

On a day when Florida State honored its 1993 national title team in a pregame ceremony, the 2013 edition of the Seminoles continued its dominant march toward a potential trip to the BCS National Championship Game in Pasadena with a 59-3 dismantling of Syracuse.

"That's one of the best football teams I've seen in my 23 years coaching," said Syracuse coach Scott Shafer. "They are big, they are fast, they are talented and they know what they're doing."

No. 2 FSU was relentless in securing its 10th victory of the season and moving to 8-0 in the ACC for the first time since 2000. The Seminoles raced to a 28-0 first-quarter lead, didn't face a third-down situation until 5:28 left in the second quarter and held the Orange to just 3.2 yards per play.

Quarterback Jameis Winston needed just two quarters of play to complete 19 of 21 passes for 277 yards and two touchdowns — and no turnovers.

"I thought Jameis played exceptionally well," said FSU coach Jimbo Fisher. "He made good decisions, got the ball where he had to get it to and got it to guys coming in and out of the right runs and checks. I thought he played a very efficient game today."

Sean Maguire, who stepped into the role of No. 2 quarterback, played the entire second half — the most on-field action of his career — and kept the offense moving.

Maguire finished 3 of 5 passing for 21 yards with his first career touchdown pass, and in the process Florida State became the first team in ACC history to score at least 40 points in 10 consecutive games.

James Wilder Jr. was responsible for 12 of those points, scoring on touchdown runs of 3 yards in the first quarter and a career-long 37 yards in the third quarter. True freshman speedster Kermit Whitfield also added a 74-yard first-quarter touchdown dash in which a downfield diving block by Winston helped spring the rookie for the stretch run to the end zone.

The Seminoles also got rushing scores from Devonta Freeman, while Kelvin Benjamin and Rashad Greene also added touchdown catches. Nick O'Leary caught a 19-yard scoring pass from Maguire to set the FSU school record for career touchdowns by a tight end with 11.

"Sean made a beautiful throw," said Fisher about the record-breaking scoring toss to O'Leary. "You can see some of Sean's talent. Sean has arm talent, he just needs reps."

Karlos Williams led the way on the ground with 78 yards on just four carries for a 19.5 yards-per-carry average, while Kenny Shaw caught seven passes for a game-high 99 yards. In total, the Seminoles racked up 523 yards — 298 through the air and 225 on the ground — despite a 41:42 to 18:18 time-of-possession edge in favor of Syracuse.

As has been the case nearly almost all season, FSU's defense was just as stellar as its offense.

The 'Noles forced two turnovers — its fifth consecutive game with more than one takeaway — when Chris

Kelvin Benjamin celebrates his 18-yard touchdown reception with an offensive lineman.

GAME 10 • NOV. 16, 2013

FLORIDA STATE 59
SYRACUSE 3

	1	2	3	4	F
Syracuse	0	0	0	3	3
Florida State	28	10	21	0	59

On a day when Florida State honored its 1993 national title team in a pregame ceremony, the 2013 edition of the Seminoles continued its dominant march toward a potential trip to the BCS National Championship Game in Pasadena with a 59-3 dismantling of Syracuse.

"That's one of the best football teams I've seen in my 23 years coaching," said Syracuse coach Scott Shafer. "They are big, they are fast, they are talented and they know what they're doing."

No. 2 FSU was relentless in securing its 10th victory of the season and moving to 8-0 in the ACC for the first time since 2000. The Seminoles raced to a 28-0 first-quarter lead, didn't face a third-down situation until 5:28 left in the second quarter and held the Orange to just 3.2 yards per play.

Quarterback Jameis Winston needed just two quarters of play to complete 19 of 21 passes for 277 yards and two touchdowns — and no turnovers.

"I thought Jameis played exceptionally well," said FSU coach Jimbo Fisher. "He made good decisions, got the ball where he had to get it to and got it to guys coming in and out of the right runs and checks. I thought he played a very efficient game today."

Sean Maguire, who stepped into the role of No. 2 quarterback, played the entire second half — the most on-field action of his career — and kept the offense moving.

Maguire finished 3 of 5 passing for 21 yards with his first career touchdown pass, and in the process Florida State became the first team in ACC history to score at least 40 points in 10 consecutive games.

James Wilder Jr. was responsible for 12 of those points, scoring on touchdown runs of 3 yards in the first quarter and a career-long 37 yards in the third quarter. True freshman speedster Kermit Whitfield also added a 74-yard first-quarter touchdown dash in which a downfield diving block by Winston helped spring the rookie for the stretch run to the end zone.

The Seminoles also got rushing scores from Devonta Freeman, while Kelvin Benjamin and Rashad Greene also added touchdown catches. Nick O'Leary caught a 19-yard scoring pass from Maguire to set the FSU school record for career touchdowns by a tight end with 11.

"Sean made a beautiful throw," said Fisher about the record-breaking scoring toss to O'Leary. "You can see some of Sean's talent. Sean has arm talent, he just needs reps."

Karlos Williams led the way on the ground with 78 yards on just four carries for a 19.5 yards-per-carry average, while Kenny Shaw caught seven passes for a game-high 99 yards. In total, the Seminoles racked up 523 yards — 298 through the air and 225 on the ground — despite a 41:42 to 18:18 time-of-possession edge in favor of Syracuse.

As has been the case nearly almost all season, FSU's defense was just as stellar as its offense.

The 'Noles forced two turnovers — its fifth consecutive game with more than one takeaway — when Chris

Casher stripped Syracuse backup quarterback Drew Allen and scooped and scored from 31 yards out, and then Dan Hicks intercepted a pass on the next Orange drive.

Syracuse was averaging more than 200 yards rushing per game, but the 'Noles stymied that attack, limiting the visitors to 143 yards on the ground (139 of which occurred in the final two quarters against the second- and third-team FSU defense). The Orange finished with just 247 yards.

Sophomore Reggie Northrup picked up a game-high 11 tackles while E.J. Levenberry, Lamarcus Brutus, Nate Andrews and Timmy Jernigan each had six stops. Dan Hicks added five tackles to his interception, and Terrance Smith also had five tackles.

Defensive back Lamarcus Joyner added to his team-high sack total with two more in the victory.

Roberto Aguayo posted a career-long 53-yard field goal to cap off the Seminoles' complete domination.

SCORING SUMMARY

First Quarter
FS	12:29	TD	Wilder 3-yd rush (Aguayo kick)
FS	10:41	TD	Whitfield 74-yd rush (Aguayo kick)
FS	4:41	TD	Freeman 4-yd rush (Aguayo kick)
FS	:40	TD	Greene 6-yd pass (Aguayo kick)

Second Quarter
FS	11:52	TD	Benjamin 6-yd pass (Aguayo kick)
FS	5:07	FG	Aguayo 53-yd

Third Quarter
FS	10:51	TD	Wilder 37-yd rush (Aguayo kick)
FS	7:45	TD	O'Leary 17-yd pass (Aguayo kick)
FS	5:47	TD	Casher 31-yd fumble rec (Aguayo kick)

Fourth Quarter
SU	7:42	FG	Norton 32-yd

FLORIDA STATE STATS

Passing
Name	Comp-Att-Int	Yards	TD
Jameis Winston	19-21-0	277	2
Sean Maguire	3-5-1	21	1
Total	22-26-1	298	3

Rushing
Name	Att-Yards	Avg	TD
Karlos Williams	4-78	19.5	0
Kermit Whitfield	1-74	74.0	1
James Wilder Jr.	3-52	17.3	2
Devonta Freeman	4-29	7.3	1
Chad Abram	1-2	2.0	0
Ryan Green	1-2	2.0	0
Jameis Winston	5-(-12)	-2.4	0
Total	19-225	11.8	4

Receiving
Name	Att-Yards	Avg	TD
Kenny Shaw	7-99	14.1	0
Kelvin Benjamin	6-66	11.0	1
Nick O'Leary	3-55	18.3	1
Rashad Greene	4-40	10.0	1
Devonta Freeman	1-34	34.0	0
Kermit Whitfield	1-4	4.0	0
Total	22-298	13.5	3

Devonta Freeman crosses the goal line on a 4-yard touchdown run in the first quarter against Syracuse.

FLORIDA STATE 59 · SYRACUSE 3

Rashad Greene goes up to snag a 6-yard touchdown pass from Jameis Winston in the first quarter.

Kelvin Benjamin looks to run after a reception. Benjamin finished with six catches for 66 yards and one touchdown.

Chris Casher returns a fumble recovery 31 yards for a touchdown.

GAME 10 · NOV. 16, 2013

Karlos Williams leaps over a defender for a few of his 78 rushing yards.

FLORIDA STATE 59 · SYRACUSE 3

Nick O'Leary caught three passes for 55 yards and one touchdown, thus setting the FSU school record for career touchdowns by a tight end with 11.

GAME 11 • NOV. 23, 2013

FLORIDA STATE 80
IDAHO 14

	1	2	3	4	F
Idaho	0	7	0	7	14
Florida State	21	21	17	21	80

No. 2 Florida State sent its seniors off in style, setting a school record for points scored in a game in an 80-14 victory over Idaho.

The 11-0 Seminoles officially broke the 18-year-old record after linebacker E.J. Levenberry ran back an interception 78 yards for a touchdown with less than five minutes to play in the game.

While a rookie capped off the dominating performance, several 'Noles playing in their final game at Doak Campbell Stadium got it all started. Wide receiver Kenny Shaw registered his first 100-yard game of the season, linebacker Telvin Smith had a highlight-reel 79-yard interception return and defensive tackle Jacobbi McDaniel picked off the second pass of his career — all of which occurred in a 42-7 first half.

Of course, Levenberry and the rest of the younger players did their part in making plays, too.

Jameis Winston continued his stellar season, despite once again not having to play an entire game. The redshirt freshman played in just the first two quarters and one series in the second half — a short final drive that concluded with a rocket-armed 21-yard strike to Kelvin Benjamin in the end zone.

Winston finished the game 14 of 25 passing for 225 yards and four touchdowns, moving to within one scoring pass of tying Chris Weinke's school-record 33 touchdown tosses in 2000.

Benjamin grabbed two of those scores, as he also had a 32-yard touchdown catch in the first quarter and finished with three grabs for 61 yards. Shaw had 107 yards and two touchdowns after coming within 11 yards of hitting the century mark in six previous games.

The 'Noles three-headed monster at tailback did work on the ground as well. Devonta Freeman took all the carries in the first quarter and finished the day with 11 runs for a season-high 129 yards and a 60-yard first-quarter score. James Wilder Jr. only had to carry four times — the quartet of carries all taking place on the same second-quarter drive — and finished with 85 yards and one touchdown. Karlos Williams came on in the second half and added 114 yards on just 10 carries.

True freshman Ryan Green ran six times for 32 yards and added a 2-yard touchdown catch from Sean Maguire in the fourth quarter. Maguire finished 9 of 14 for 84 yards with one touchdown and one interception.

The Seminoles were remarkably balanced in the win, rushing for 336 yards and passing for 309. The 'Noles' 645 total yards were a season high and marked the third time this year they eclipsed 600 yards.

With 607 total points in 2013, Florida State set a school and ACC record for most points in a year, breaking the short-lived record of 550 the Seminoles set in 2012. FSU also set a new conference record for most touchdowns in a year with 80, breaking the 1995 FSU team's previous benchmark of 72.

Defensively, FSU continued its dominance. Led by star junior nose guard Timmy Jernigan, the Seminoles had a season-best eight sacks. Jernigan finished with 2

1/2 of those sacks while adding 4 1/2 tackles for loss and six total stops in just a first half of play.

Already the nation's leader in total interceptions, FSU's defense padded those stats against the Vandals with four more interceptions to push their 11-game total to 23. In addition to McDaniel, Smith and Levenberry, true freshman Marquez White also intercepted a pass. Sixteen different 'Noles now have an interception this season, and for comparison's sake, 14 different players have catches on the offensive side of the football.

Senior Lamarcus Joyner and Smith both finished with four tackles while DeMarcus Walker, Derrick Mitchell, Eddie Goldman, Dan Hicks and Desmond Hollin were all involved in FSU's sack total.

Not to be outdone, Roberto Aguayo continued his sensational kicking. Agauyo set the national record for consecutive made extra points when he drilled his 78th point-after of the season early in the fourth quarter, making him 80 for 80 on the season.

SCORING SUMMARY

First Quarter
FS	9:58	TD	Freeman 60-yd rush (Aguayo kick)
FS	5:18	TD	Benjamin 32-yd pass (Aguayo kick)
FS	3:05	TD	Smith 79-yd INT (Aguayo kick)

Second Quarter
FS	12:48	TD	Shaw 46-yd pass (Aguayo kick)
FS	5:54	TD	Wilder 1-yd rush (Aguayo kick)
UI	:41	TD	Montgomery 15-yd pass (Rehkow kick)
FS	:04	TD	Shaw 20-yd pass (Aguayo kick)

Third Quarter
FS	13:11	TD	Benjamin 21-yd pass (Aguayo kick)
FS	11:34	TD	Williams 4-yd rush (Aguayo kick)
FS	3:07	FG	Aguayo 42-yd

Fourth Quarter
FS	14:25	TD	Williams 25-yd rush (Aguayo kick)
FS	7:18	TD	Green 2-yd pass (Aguayo kick)
FS	4:19	TD	Levenberry 78-yd INT (Aguayo kick)
UI	:42	TD	Lovett 14-yd pass (Rehkow kick)

FLORIDA STATE STATS

Passing
Name	Comp-Att-Int	Yards	TD
Jameis Winston	14-25-0	225	4
Sean Maguire	9-14-1	84	1
Total	23-39-1	309	5

Rushing
Name	Att-Yards	Avg	TD
Devonta Freeman	11-129	11.7	1
Karlos Williams	10-114	11.4	2
James Wilder Jr.	4-85	21.3	1
Ryan Green	6-32	5.3	0
Freddie Stevenson	2-7	3.5	0
Will Burnham	1-6	6.0	0
Kermit Whitfield	1-5	5.0	0
Jameis Winston	4-(-19)	-4.8	0
TEAM	1-(-23)	-23.0	0
Total	40-336	8.4	4

Receiving
Name	Att-Yards	Avg	TD
Kenny Shaw	5-107	21.4	2
Kelvin Benjamin	3-61	20.3	2
Christian Green	2-31	15.5	0
Rashad Greene	3-29	9.7	0
Karlos Williams	2-17	8.5	0
Ryan Green	2-16	8.0	1
Nick O'Leary	1-13	13.0	0
Jesus Wilson	2-(12)	6.0	0
Chad Abram	1-(9)	9.0	0
Freddie Stevenson	1-8	8.0	0
Devonta Freeman	1-6	6.0	0
Total	23-309	13.4	5

Nobody could catch Devonta Freeman on a 60-yard touchdown run in the first quarter. Freeman finished with 129 yards on 11 carries.

FLORIDA STATE 80 · IDAHO 14

Linebacker Telvin Smith (22) runs back an interception 79 yards for a touchdown.

Mario Edwards Jr. welcomes the Idaho quarterback to Tallahassee.

James Wilder Jr. fights off a defender. Wilder had 85 yards on four carries with one touchdown.

Jameis Winston unleashes a pass. Playing just a little over two quarters, the freshman threw four touchdown passes.

FLORIDA STATE 80 • IDAHO 14

The Marching Chiefs had a lot to smile about during the game.

GAME 12 • NOV. 30, 2013

FLORIDA STATE 37
FLORIDA 7

	1	2	3	4	F
Florida State	3	14	10	10	37
Florida	0	0	0	7	7

Florida State continued its undefeated roll as the Seminoles scored the game's first 27 points and pummeled their cross-state rival Florida 37-7. The 'Noles finished the regular season with a 12-0 record for the first time since 1999.

The 30-point margin of victory for FSU was the largest by the Seminoles over Florida in Gainesville.

Kelvin Benjamin led the way for the 'Noles as he caught nine Jameis Winston passes for a career-high 212 yards and three touchdowns, including a pair in the second quarter.

"KB has real advantages with his size, speed and athleticism," said Florida State head coach Jimbo Fisher about Benjamin's effort. "He can be a very, very special player, and he's starting to develop into that guy."

Winston was 19 of 31 passing for 327 yards and the three touchdown tosses to Benjamin as he became the first quarterback in over three years to throw for 300 or more yards against the Gators. In the process, Winston set the FSU record for season touchdown passes with 35, formerly held by Chris Weinke, who had 33 scoring passes in his Heisman Trophy senior season of 2000.

Winston was intercepted deep in Florida territory early in the game, but the Gators missed a chance to take the lead when Austin Hardin missed a 49-yard field goal. Florida State went back to work, and Roberto Aguayo connected on a 49-yarder of his own for a 3-0 FSU lead with 3:43 left in the first quarter.

A Florida punt pinned the 'Noles deep in their territory in the second quarter, but Winston led FSU on a 12-play, 96-yard march, capped off by a 45-yard touchdown catch by Benjamin and a 10-0 Seminoles lead with 4:24 to play.

Florida State's defense continued to plague the Gators as the 'Noles forced a three-and-out, and FSU took over at its 26-yard line. Winston completed five of six passes in the drive, the last a 29-yarder to Benjamin down the sideline with 25 seconds to go in the half, as the Seminoles took a 17-0 advantage.

Winston threw for 208 yards in the first half for the third straight game and the eighth time in the 2013 season. The FSU defense allowed just three first downs to the Gators in the first two quarters.

Florida freshman quarterback Skyler Mornhinweg was sacked by defensive end Mario Edwards Jr. on the Gators' first play from scrimmage in the second half. Edwards stripped the ball away, and linebacker Telvin Smith recovered at the Florida 39. It was the 17th consecutive game that the Seminoles forced a turnover.

Six plays later, Florida State turned Florida's miscue into points as Aguayo made his second field goal, a 40-yarder, for a 20-0 lead just four minutes into the third quarter.

Devonta Freeman added an 11-yard touchdown run with 7:08 left in the third quarter as FSU extended the margin to 27-0.

The Marching Chiefs had a lot to smile about during the game.

GAME 12 • NOV. 30, 2013

FLORIDA STATE 37
FLORIDA 7

	1	2	3	4	F
Florida State	3	14	10	10	37
Florida	0	0	0	7	7

Florida State continued its undefeated roll as the Seminoles scored the game's first 27 points and pummeled their cross-state rival Florida 37-7. The 'Noles finished the regular season with a 12-0 record for the first time since 1999.

The 30-point margin of victory for FSU was the largest by the Seminoles over Florida in Gainesville.

Kelvin Benjamin led the way for the 'Noles as he caught nine Jameis Winston passes for a career-high 212 yards and three touchdowns, including a pair in the second quarter.

"KB has real advantages with his size, speed and athleticism," said Florida State head coach Jimbo Fisher about Benjamin's effort. "He can be a very, very special player, and he's starting to develop into that guy."

Winston was 19 of 31 passing for 327 yards and the three touchdown tosses to Benjamin as he became the first quarterback in over three years to throw for 300 or more yards against the Gators. In the process, Winston set the FSU record for season touchdown passes with 35, formerly held by Chris Weinke, who had 33 scoring passes in his Heisman Trophy senior season of 2000.

Winston was intercepted deep in Florida territory early in the game, but the Gators missed a chance to take the lead when Austin Hardin missed a 49-yard field goal. Florida State went back to work, and Roberto Aguayo connected on a 49-yarder of his own for a 3-0 FSU lead with 3:43 left in the first quarter.

A Florida punt pinned the 'Noles deep in their territory in the second quarter, but Winston led FSU on a 12-play, 96-yard march, capped off by a 45-yard touchdown catch by Benjamin and a 10-0 Seminoles lead with 4:24 to play.

Florida State's defense continued to plague the Gators as the 'Noles forced a three-and-out, and FSU took over at its 26-yard line. Winston completed five of six passes in the drive, the last a 29-yarder to Benjamin down the sideline with 25 seconds to go in the half, as the Seminoles took a 17-0 advantage.

Winston threw for 208 yards in the first half for the third straight game and the eighth time in the 2013 season. The FSU defense allowed just three first downs to the Gators in the first two quarters.

Florida freshman quarterback Skyler Mornhinweg was sacked by defensive end Mario Edwards Jr. on the Gators' first play from scrimmage in the second half. Edwards stripped the ball away, and linebacker Telvin Smith recovered at the Florida 39. It was the 17th consecutive game that the Seminoles forced a turnover.

Six plays later, Florida State turned Florida's miscue into points as Aguayo made his second field goal, a 40-yarder, for a 20-0 lead just four minutes into the third quarter.

Devonta Freeman added an 11-yard touchdown run with 7:08 left in the third quarter as FSU extended the margin to 27-0.

Florida finally got on the scoreboard with 13:39 to play in the fourth quarter when Mornhinweg threw a 5-yard touchdown pass to fullback Hunter Joyer.

The Seminoles responded with a 10-play, 79-yard drive as FSU used five runs by James Wilder Jr. mixed in with Winston's arm and feet. Winston extended the drive twice with completed third-down passes to Benjamin and Rashad Greene, and on third and goal at the Florida 4, threw his third scoring pass of the game to Benjamin for a 34-7 lead with 8:06 remaining.

Mornhinweg fumbled again on Florida's next possession, and FSU's Nate Andrews recovered at the Gators 32. Aguayo's 28-yard field goal with 3:14 to play completed the scoring.

The Seminoles' defense held the Gators to 193 total yards of offense, an average of 3.9 yards per play, and eight first downs.

Greene caught four passes for 25 yards while Nick O'Leary added three catches for 52 yards as he moved into a tie for second place in career receptions by a FSU tight end.

P.J. Williams, Christian Jones, Lamarcus Joyner and Terrence Brooks each had five total tackles for the Seminoles' defensive unit. Two of Jones' and Brooks' tackles each were for loss, as the 'Noles had seven tackles behind the Gators' line of scrimmage.

SCORING SUMMARY

First Quarter
FSU 3:43 FG Aguayo 49-yd

Second Quarter
FSU 4:24 TD Benjamin 45-yd pass (Aguayo kick)
FSU :25   TD Benjamin 29-yd pass (Aguayo kick)

Third Quarter
FSU 11:02 FG Aguayo 40-yd
FSU 7:08   TD Freeman 11-yd rush (Aguayo kick)

Fourth Quarter
UF   13:39 TD Joyer 5-yd pass (Velez kick)
FSU 8:06   TD Benjamin 4-yd pass (Aguayo kick)
FSU 3:14   FG Aguayo 28-yd

FLORIDA STATE STATS

Passing
Name	Comp-Att-Int	Yards	TD
Jameis Winston	19-31-1	327	3
Total	19-31-1	327	3

Rushing
Name	Att-Yards	Avg	TD
James Wilder Jr.	10-63	6.3	0
Devonta Freeman	13-44	3.4	1
Karlos Williams	4-14	3.5	0
Jameis Winston	5-8	1.6	0
Total	32-129	4.0	1

Receiving
Name	Att-Yards	Avg	TD
Kelvin Benjamin	9-212	23.6	3
Nick O'Leary	3-52	17.3	0
Kenny Shaw	1-27	27.0	0
Rashad Greene	4-25	6.3	0
Devonta Freeman	2-11	5.5	0
Total	19-327	17.2	3

Kelvin Benjamin refused to go down while scoring FSU's first touchdown against Florida.

FLORIDA STATE 37 · FLORIDA 7

Timmy Jernigan (8) and Nile Lawrence-Stample collect a tackle for loss.

Nick O'Leary goes high to snare a pass. O'Leary caught three balls for 52 yards.

FLORIDA STATE 37 · FLORIDA 7

Eddie Goldman sacks the Gators quarterback.

Kelvin Benjamin hauls in one of his nine receptions for 212 yards and three touchdowns.

FLORIDA STATE 37 · FLORIDA 7

With a perfect 12-0 regular-season record after the victory, the Seminoles and head coach Jimbo Fisher were headed to the ACC Championship Game.

GAME 13 • DEC. 7, 2013

FLORIDA STATE 45
DUKE 7

	1	2	3	4	F
Florida State	0	17	21	7	45
Duke	0	0	0	7	7

For the 14th time in program history, Florida State became champions of the Atlantic Coast Conference. The 45-7 victory over No. 20 Duke was the final hurdle to a date in the BCS National Championship Game.

"Very happy for our team, our university," said FSU head coach Jimbo Fisher. "This championship means a lot to us. This is where we want to be every year, and we have to get here to keep achieving and going to BCS games and the other games in which we want to get to, but the ultimate goal is to always win your conference, and I think this conference is a great conference."

FSU (13-0) punched its ticket to Pasadena with yet another blowout victory built on an explosive offense and a dominating defense. The 'Noles outgained the Blue Devils 569-239 in Charlotte.

FSU redshirt freshman quarterback Jameis Winston beat Duke with his arm and legs. Winston finished the night 19 of 32 passing for 320 yards, three touchdowns and two interceptions. He also added 61 yards rushing on nine carries and a leaping score.

In the process, Winston set the single-season record for the ACC and among FBS freshmen for passing touchdowns in a season and also set the FBS single-season passing-yardage record among freshmen.

For his efforts against Duke, Winston was named the ACC Championship Game MVP.

Kelvin Benjamin continued his stellar play, catching five of Winston's passes for a game-high 111 yards with two touchdowns. Rashad Greene finished with 66 yards on six grabs and Kenny Shaw caught four for 73 yards.

Devonta Freeman gained 95 yards against Duke on 17 carries with one touchdown. Karlos Williams added 58 yards and a touchdown of his own.

Of course, Florida State's defense was just as impressive as its offense.

Duke had just 99 yards rushing and was held to 7 of 20 on third downs. Duke quarterback Anthony Boone was limited to 138 yards through the air and was intercepted twice — by Lamarcus Joyner and Telvin Smith.

Timmy Jernigan had another monster game from his nose guard position, racking up a game-best 10 tackles. Smith finished with eight tackles, a sack and that takeaway, while Nate Andrews had five stops, a sack and a forced fumble.

The first big play of the night went Duke's way when Freeman fumbled at the end of a 22-yard dash into the redzone early in the first quarter.

After taking over at their own 3, the Blue Devils strung together an impressive 6:03 drive into FSU territory but shanked a 48-yard field goal that would have put FSU into a deficit for the first time since September.

Winston needed just five plays to find a leaping Benjamin in the end zone for the game's first score. Leading 7-0, Duke registered a 40-yard punt return into FSU territory two drives later, but a Joyner interception halted any hopes the Blue Devils had of getting on the board.

The Joyner turnover would then turn into points. Freeman's impressive 22-yard reception was followed by a big Benjamin third-down conversion. Williams then came into the lineup and rumbled 12 yards for the touchdown and a 14-0 FSU lead with 3:37 left in the second quarter.

FSU's Roberto Aguayo then connected on a 45-yard field goal with 33 seconds left in the half that pushed Florida State's lead to 17-0 heading into the break.

After Andrews' big hit on Boone forced the Duke quarterback to throw a bad pass that was intercepted by Smith, Winston connected with Shaw for an 11-yard scoring strike to give FSU a 24-0 lead.

Winston then threw a 54-yard touchdown to Benjamin on the next drive. If that wasn't enough, Winston then added to his record-breaking night with a 17-yard touchdown run — his fourth score — one drive later that tied the ACC title-game mark for most touchdowns by one player.

On his final drive of the night, Winston orchestrated one last scoring possession that concluded with a 7-yard Freeman touchdown run.

Duke avoided the shutout by marching 75 yards against the FSU second-team defense.

SCORING SUMMARY

Second Quarter
FSU	12:36	TD	Benjamin 14-yd pass (Aguayo kick)
FSU	3:37	TD	Williams 12-yd rush (Aguayo kick)
FSU	:25	FG	Aguayo 45-yd

Third Quarter
FSU	9:52	TD	Shaw 11-yd pass (Aguayo kick)
FSU	6:31	TD	Benjamin 46-yd pass (Aguayo kick)
FSU	2:38	TD	Winston 17-yd rush (Aguayo kick)

Fourth Quarter
FSU	7:25	TD	Freeman 7-yd rush (Aguayo kick)
DU	1:01	TD	Snead 5-yd rush (Martin kick)

FLORIDA STATE STATS

Passing
Name	Comp-Att-Int	Yards	TD
Jameis Winston	19-32-2	320	3
Total	19-32-2	320	3

Rushing
Name	Att-Yards	Avg	TD
Devonta Freeman	17-95	5.6	1
Jameis Winston	9-61	6.8	1
Karlos Williams	9-58	6.4	1
James Wilder Jr.	5-25	5.0	0
Freddie Stevenson	1-2	2.0	0
Chad Abram	1-2	2.0	0
Ryan Green	1-1	1.0	0
Total	43-244	5.7	3

Receiving
Name	Att-Yards	Avg	TD
Kelvin Benjamin	5-111	22.2	2
Kenny Shaw	4-73	18.3	1
Rashad Greene	6-66	11.0	0
Nick O'Leary	3-48	16.0	0
Devonta Freeman	1-22	22.0	0
Total	19-320	16.8	3

Jameis Winston unleashes a touchdown pass to Kelvin Benjamin against Duke. Winston completed 19 of 32 attempts for 320 yards and three touchdowns.

Kelvin Benjamin eludes a Duke tackler. Benjamin finished with five catches for 111 yards and two touchdowns.

Karlos Williams scores FSU's second touchdown behind Devonta Freeman's block.

Devonta Freeman breaks a tackle against the Blue Devils. Freeman led the Seminoles in rushing with 95 yards and one touchdown.

Jameis Winston scores on a 17-yard run late in the third quarter.

Devonta Freeman breaks a tackle against the Blue Devils. Freeman led the Seminoles in rushing with 95 yards and one touchdown.

Jameis Winston scores on a 17-yard run late in the third quarter.

Devonta Freeman breaks a tackle against the Blue Devils. Freeman led the Seminoles in rushing with 95 yards and one touchdown.

Jameis Winston scores on a 17-yard run late in the third quarter.

Devonta Freeman breaks a tackle against the Blue Devils. Freeman led the Seminoles in rushing with 95 yards and one touchdown.

Jameis Winston scores on a 17-yard run late in the third quarter.

FLORIDA STATE 45 · DUKE 7

Nate Andrews knocks down a Duke pass. The freshman defensive back also had five tackles, a sack and a forced fumble in Charlotte.

GAME 13 · DEC. 7, 2013

James Wilder Jr. breaks through the Duke defensive line.

Bryan Stork raises a piece of Bank of America Stadium sod, which was ceremoniously inducted into FSU's Sod Cemetery in Tallahassee.

FLORIDA STATE 45 · DUKE 7

Head coach Jimbo Fisher celebrates winning the 2013 ACC Championship Game.

FLORIDA STATE 45 · DUKE 7

GAME 14: BCS NATIONAL CHAMPIONSHIP GAME • JAN. 6, 2014
FLORIDA STATE 34
AUBURN 31

	1	2	3	4	F
Florida State	3	7	3	21	34
Auburn	7	14	0	10	31

The No. 1 Seminoles flipped a month-long narrative on its ear, and in the process, ended a seven-year streak of Southeastern Conference dominance as Florida State won its third national championship.

In thrilling fashion, Florida State's come-from-behind 34-31 triumph over Auburn at the Rose Bowl in Pasadena silenced a nation of critics, who cited the Seminoles' lack of close games in 2013 as being a significant weakness in the highly anticipated California clash of southern football powers. From the time the pairings were decided in early December, the running dialogue about the final BCS National Championship Game was that the ACC champions weren't battle tested and therefore vulnerable to the grittier SEC champion Tigers, who had made magic in close games all year long.

Prior to the national title game, FSU's version of adversity had been a 17-3 deficit in late September at Boston College in which they skillfully navigated and emerged victorious. FSU hadn't trailed in a game since that trek to New England — a whopping 538 minutes of consecutive game action — before Auburn raced to a 21-3 lead in front of 94,000-plus fans and an entire nation watching.

Looking doomed defensively and uncharacteristically uncoordinated offensively, the 'Noles naysayers seemed to be well on their way to an accurate prediction.

But while the Seminoles hadn't experienced the pressures of battling from an 18-point hole during the season, that didn't mean that they hadn't prepared for such a scenario.

"We were down but we practice that situation every day to end off practice," said FSU tailback James Wilder Jr. "It wasn't nothing we weren't actually prepared for, so I mean we just came out there, [and] everybody still loved each other and still believed in each other, and we came out victorious."

After Tre Mason recaptured Auburn's lead it had relinquished to the second-half surging 'Noles on a 37-yard scoring run, FSU maintained its composure. Despite there being just 1:19 separating them from a title-game loss, Jameis Winston and the offense calmly orchestrated what would turn out to be the game-winning scoring drive that was highlighted by Kelvin Benjamin's leaping 2-yard touchdown grab with 13 seconds remaining.

Winston capped off one of the greatest seasons by any player ever with that defining drive, locating his open receivers, traversing the dwindling clock and ultimately making the perfect throw to the perfect person in that particular situation for the win.

"You've got to be 'G.U.M.P.' — great under major pressure — and that's what I love about him," FSU tailback Devonta Freeman said about his quarterback.

Were the Seminoles battle tested before Auburn? Certainly not. But their ability to handle adversity and conquer it helped them win the fight and ultimately the war against the SEC's seven-season championship streak.

"We heard what was being said about us all week," said FSU defensive tackle Jacobbi McDaniel. "Nobody thought we could win if we had to fight to do it. We always knew what we were capable of and now everybody else knows."

After Roberto Aguayo opened the scoring with a 35-yard field goal in the first quarter, Auburn scored the next 21 points for a 21-3 advantage with 5:01 to play in the second quarter. Freeman scored on a 3-yard run with 1:28 to play to cut the Tigers' halftime lead to 21-10.

An Aguayo 41-yard field goal provided the only points of the third quarter as FSU trailed 21-13.

A furious fourth quarter started with a 11-yard touchdown catch by Chad Abram with 10:55 remaining as FSU pulled within 21-20. Auburn pushed its lead to 24-20 on a field goal with 4:42 left. On the ensuing kickoff, Florida State's Kermit Whitfield returned the kick 100 yards for a touchdown and a 27-24 lead.

Auburn drove 75 yards in 3:12 to take the lead on Mason's second touchdown, but Florida State marched 80 yards in seven plays to bring the national championship back to Tallahassee.

Winston was named the Offensive Player of the Game after completing 20 of 35 passes for 237 yards and two touchdowns. He also rushed 11 times for 26 yards. Defensive back P.J. Williams was the contest's Defensive Player of the Game after posting seven total tackles and an interception.

SCORING SUMMARY

First Quarter
FS	9:53	FG	Aguayo 35-yd
AU	3:07	TD	Mason 12-yd pass (Parkey kick)

Second Quarter
AU	13:48	TD	Ray 50-yd pass (Parkey kick)
AU	5:01	TD	Marshall 4-yd rush (Parkey kick)
FS	1:28	TD	Freeman 3-yd rush (Aguayo kick)

Third Quarter
FS	6:05	FG	Aguayo 41-yd

Fourth Quarter
FS	10:55	TD	Abram 11-yd pass (Aguayo kick)
AU	4:42	FG	Parkey 22-yd
FS	4:31	TD	Whitfield 100-yd KO ret (Aguayo kick)
AU	1:19	TD	Mason 37-yd rush (Parkey kick)
FS	:13	TD	Benjamin 2-yd pass (Aguayo kick)

FLORIDA STATE STATS

Passing
Name	Comp-Att-Int	Yards	TD
Jameis Winston	20-35-0	237	2
Total	20-35-0	237	2

Rushing
Name	Att-Yards	Avg	TD
Devonta Freeman	11-73	6.6	1
Jameis Winston	11-26	2.4	0
Karlos Williams	5-25	5.0	0
James Wilder Jr.	3-21	7.0	0
Chad Abram	1-3	3.0	0
Total	31-148	4.8	1

Receiving
Name	Att-Yards	Avg	TD
Rashad Greene	9-147	16.3	0
Kelvin Benjamin	4-54	13.5	1
Devonta Freeman	3-21	7.0	0
Chad Abram	1-11	11.0	1
Kenny Shaw	2-4	2.0	0
Karlos Williams	1-0	0.0	0
Total	20-237	11.8	2

Head coach Jimbo Fisher makes a point to his players in the locker room before the BCS National Championship Game in Pasadena, California.

Osceola and Renegade lead the Seminoles onto the Rose Bowl field prior to kickoff.

FLORIDA STATE 34 · AUBURN 31

The Marching Chiefs' drum major plants his baton before the game.

GAME 14: BCS NATIONAL CHAMPIONSHIP GAME · JAN. 6, 2014

James Wilder Jr. (left) and Devonta Freeman celebrate Freeman's 3-yard touchdown run late in the second quarter.

Chad Abram goes over an Auburn defender for an 11-yard touchdown reception.

GAME 14: BCS NATIONAL CHAMPIONSHIP GAME – JAN. 6, 2014

Head coach Jimbo Fisher and quarterback coach Randy Sanders try to get someone's attention on the field.

FLORIDA STATE 34 · AUBURN 31

P.J. Williams (26) and Jalen Ramsey tackle Auburn running back Tre Mason.

GAME 14: BCS NATIONAL CHAMPIONSHIP GAME · JAN. 6, 2014

Mario Edwards Jr. brings down Auburn quarterback Nick Marshall.

FLORIDA STATE 34 · AUBURN 31

GAME 14: BCS NATIONAL CHAMPIONSHIP GAME · JAN. 6, 2014

Kermit Whitfield flies down the field on a 100-yard kickoff return for a touchdown with 4:31 remaining in the game.

Jameis Winston looks for room to run against the Tigers.

GAME 14: BCS NATIONAL CHAMPIONSHIP GAME · JAN. 6, 2014

Christian Jones (7), Timmy Jernigan (8) and Mario Edwards Jr. take down Tre Mason.

FLORIDA STATE 34 · AUBURN 31

P.J. Williams picks off a Nick Marshall pass.

FLORIDA STATE 34 · AUBURN 31

GAME 14: BCS NATIONAL CHAMPIONSHIP GAME · JAN. 6, 2014

■ Chad Abram on the run in the fourth quarter.

P.J. Williams pressures Nick Marshall into throwing a bad pass.

GAME 14: BCS NATIONAL CHAMPIONSHIP GAME • JAN. 6, 2014

Karlos Williams builds up a head of steam as he attacks the Auburn defense.

Jameis Winston led the Seminoles on a furious fourth-quarter rally, scoring 21 points in the final period.

FLORIDA STATE 34 · AUBURN 31

GAME 14: BCS NATIONAL CHAMPIONSHIP GAME · JAN. 6, 2014

Rashad Greene takes off after a catch on the game-winning drive.

FLORIDA STATE 34 · AUBURN 31

Rashad Greene finished with nine receptions for 147 yards.

Kelvin Benjamin goes up to make the game-winning touchdown catch.

FSU head coach Jimbo Fisher raises the Crystal Football portion of The Coaches' Trophy after the victory.

GAME 14: BCS NATIONAL CHAMPIONSHIP GAME · JAN. 6, 2014

Coach Jimbo Fisher celebrates with the Seminoles, his son and wife (right), and Bowl Championship Series Executive Director Bill Hancock (second from left).

The Seminoles were all smiles after winning Florida State's third national championship and the first since 1999.

FLORIDA STATE 34 · AUBURN 31

ESPN's John Saunders interviews Jameis Winston, who was named Offensive Player of the Game after completing 20 of 35 pass attempts for 237 yards and two touchdowns.

GAME 14: BCS NATIONAL CHAMPIONSHIP GAME · JAN. 6, 2014

P.J. Williams was named Defensive Player of the Game after recording seven tackles and an interception.

GAME 14: BCS NATIONAL CHAMPIONSHIP GAME · JAN. 6, 2014

P.J. Williams was named Defensive Player of the Game after recording seven tackles and an interception.

FLORIDA STATE 34 · AUBURN 31

ESPN's John Saunders interviews **Jameis Winston**, who was named Offensive Player of the Game after completing 20 of 35 pass attempts for 237 yards and two touchdowns.

FLORIDA STATE 34 · AUBURN 31

Offensive tackle Cameron Erving lifts Coach Fisher off the ground during the locker room celebration after the game.

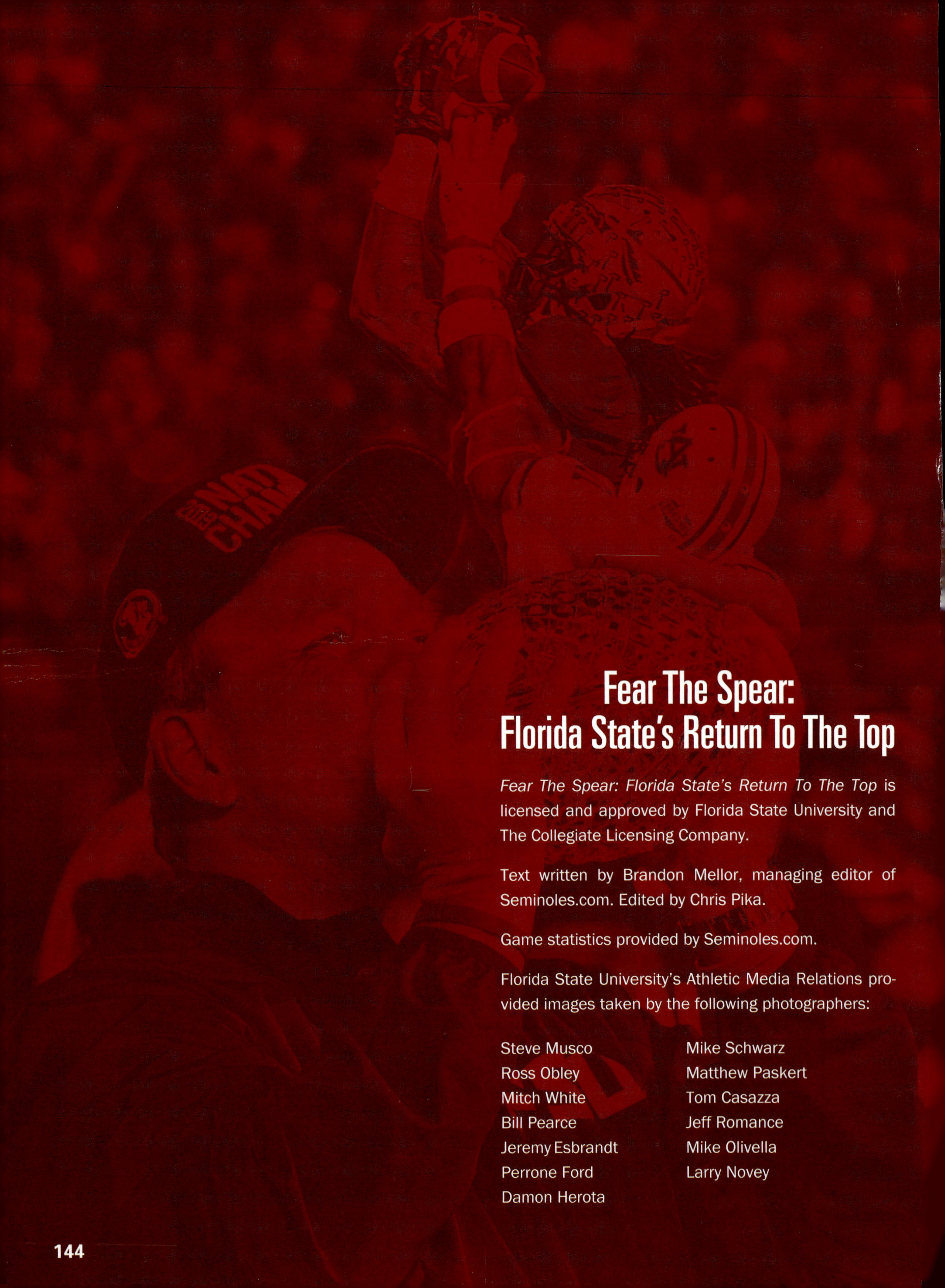

Fear The Spear: Florida State's Return To The Top

Fear The Spear: Florida State's Return To The Top is licensed and approved by Florida State University and The Collegiate Licensing Company.

Text written by Brandon Mellor, managing editor of Seminoles.com. Edited by Chris Pika.

Game statistics provided by Seminoles.com.

Florida State University's Athletic Media Relations provided images taken by the following photographers:

Steve Musco
Ross Obley
Mitch White
Bill Pearce
Jeremy Esbrandt
Perrone Ford
Damon Herota

Mike Schwarz
Matthew Paskert
Tom Casazza
Jeff Romance
Mike Olivella
Larry Novey